This is the Mass

This is
THE
MASS

as described by Henri Daniel-Rops

as celebrated by Fulton J. Sheen

as photographed by Yousuf Karsh

Translated by Alastair Guinan
With an introduction by Bishop Sheen

HAWTHORN BOOKS, INC.
Publishers · New York

Nihil obstat
JOSEPH H. BRADY, s.t.d.
CENSOR LIBRORUM

Imprimatur
THOMAS A. BOLAND, s.t.d.
ARCHBISHOP OF NEWARK
January 14, 1958

SEGRETERIA DI STATO

DI SUA SANTITA

SECRETARIATE OF STATE OF HIS HOLINESS,
THE VATICAN, 3 MAY 1952. (n.275829).

SIR:

The Holy Father has duly received the handsomely bound copy of your little work on the Mystery of the Altar, *Missa Est,* which you sent to him in a spirit of filial respect.

I am happy to tell you that he is well pleased with this book in which you continue your praiseworthy efforts to communicate, and widely to diffuse, the Christian spirit by explaining to your readers the meaning and significance of the various parts of the Mass. His Holiness trusts that your book will convey to its readers those insights which will help them to a fuller sharing in the Holy Sacrifice; and that end, doubtless, will be the best recompense the book's author could desire. The Sovereign Pontiff gladly renews, at this time, his Apostolic Blessing to you, as an expression of his paternal encouragement of your work, and of his gratitude for your filial greetings.

Be assured, Sir, of my own sincere good wishes.

J. B. MONTINI
Sostituto

MONSIEUR DANIEL-ROPS,
NEUILLY SUR SEINE.

Contents

The Sacrifice of the Mass

SOME THINGS IN LIFE are too beautiful to be forgotten. These things may be what men do in this world; they may even be their manner of passing from it. For example, almost every country has instituted a memorial day to recall the supreme sacrifice its patriots have made in defense of country and civilization. Because life was the most precious thing they could give, the living cannot forget their gift. They themselves could not ask for any such memorial, nor could they institute it; that was left to their survivors.

If it is fitting that we have memorial days for those who died to preserve freedom from the oppression of men, it is fitting, too, that there be a memorial for the supreme sacrifice of Christ Who died to give us freedom from the tyranny of sin. There are many differences, however, between those patriots and Christ. No one of them was born to die; each was born to live and death was for each a brutal interruption. But Our Lord came to die; it was the goal of His life, it was the goal He was seeking. For no other purpose came He into the world than to redeem sinful humanity.

Furthermore, unlike the men who could not make their own memorial, He instituted the precise way in which His death was to be recalled. Since He came to die, this death was the chief thing He wished us to remember. He did not say that men should write a history of it, or even that they should be kind to the poor in memory of Him; He gave them the exact manner in which He wished this sacrifice to be commemorated. The memorial He gave us is called the Mass.

It was instituted the night before He died at what has since then been called the Last Supper. Taking bread into His hands He said: "This is my body, which is to be given for you," that is, the next day on the cross. Then over the chalice of wine, He said: "This is my blood, of the new testament, which is to be shed for many to the remission of sins." He was a priest offering Himself as a victim so that men might never forget that "greater love than this no man hath than that he lay down his life for his friends." And after prefiguring and foreshadowing the way in which He would die the next day for the redemption of the world, He gave the Divine command to His Apostles and to His Church: "Do this for a commemoration of Me." In that Last Supper He looked *forward* to the Cross; in the Mass we *look back* to it.

The Mass is the application and the projection through space and time of the redemptive love of Christ on the Cross. Imagine a radio station sending out messages from all eternity, it is there all the time but we only hear the messages as we begin to tune in. So, too, the sacrifice that was offered on the Cross has an eternal value, but the Mass helps more and more people to "tune in" on its merits and to apply them to themselves.

The Redemption of Our Lord on the Cross was offered once for all, but its actualization has depended upon the unfolding of history. Potentially every human being in the world was redeemed on the cross; the actualization and the application of that redemption depends upon the free cooperation of man in the course of history.

Calvary took up only a moment of time, but being the sacrifice of the Eternal God made man, it was capable of illumining the whole of time in all periods of history. The Mass is the projection in time of the eternal values of Calvary.

Similarly Calvary was only one small place on the earth at the crossroads of Jerusalem, Athens and Rome, but what took place there, the sacrifice of the Omnipotent, can affect man everywhere in all corners of the earth. The Mass plants the cross in a town, in a village, in a mission, in a great cathedral; it draws back the curtains on time and space and makes what happened on Calvary happen there. The cross affected all past history by *anticipation;* all the sacrifices of bullocks, and goats, and sheep, and particularly the sacrifice of the paschal lamb, found their completion in the cross. The cross affected also the *future,* by flowing out through all time, like a mighty waterfall or cascade which makes channels through valleys and plains.

The very fact that all sacrifices practically ceased after the sacrifice of Calvary, meant that Calvary was the perfection and the fulfillment of *all* sacrifices. Even the Jews no longer sacrifice paschal lambs in their synagogues, for the True Paschal Lamb has already been sacrificed.

The sacrifice of the Cross, therefore, is not something that happened more than 1900 years ago, it is something that is still happening. It is not an heirloom or an antique which endures into the present; it is a drama as actual now as then, and so it will remain as long as time and eternity endure.

On the Cross Our Blessed Lord knew how every individual soul in the world would react to His supreme act of love, whether or not they would accept Him or reject Him. We ourselves do not know how we will react until we are confronted with Christ and His Cross, and we see it unrolled on the screen of time. From our point of view, it takes time to see the drama unfolded. But the Mass gives us an intimation; we were not conscious of being present on Calvary on Good Friday, but we are consciously present at the Mass. We can know something of the role we played at Calvary by the way we act at the Mass in the twentieth century, and by the way the Mass helps us to live.

The Mass is not a *new sacrifice* but another *enactment* of the one supreme sacrifice of Calvary. There are two moments in history, one when the sacrifice is expected and the other when the sacrifice is possessed and offered. The first moment is called B.C., the second moment is called A.D.

If the Blessed Mother and St. John at the foot of the Cross had closed their eyes when Our Lord was offering Himself for the sins of the world, the spiritual effects on them would have been no different from those which we may receive as we assist at the Sacrifice of the Mass. But if their eyes were open, there would have been this difference: they

11

would have seen the sacrifice offered in bloodshed with blood pouring from gaping holes in hands and feet and side. In the Mass, we see it performed without bloodshed.

The Mass, therefore, is not a substitute for the Cross, but the merit we gain at the Mass is the same as the merit we would have gained if we had assisted at Calvary.

The reason there is only one sacrifice, is that the Priest and the Victim both on the Cross and in the Mass, are one and the same person. Up until the coming of the Son of God, there were many sacrifices offered for sins. Men felt that they were unfit to exist before the Divine Presence. By taking the life of an animal or by destroying a thing, they vicariously punished and purified themselves. Among all peoples, in addition to the Jews who had the great advantage of Divine revelation, there were therefore, priests who offered victims of sacrifice. Their task was to slay the goat or the sheep, or pour out the wine, or immolate the bull. But when Our Lord came He became at one and the same time *Priest* and *Victim*, He became both the Offerer and the One Who was offered. No longer were the priest and victims *separate* as they had been before. On the Cross, therefore, He was upright as a Priest; He was prostrate as a Victim because He was offering Himself.

The Priest offers the Mass only as the representative of Christ, hence he does not say, at the moment of consecration, this is the Body and Blood of Christ but "This is My Body" and "This is My Blood;" he is only an instrument of Christ in the same way that a pencil is an instrument of one who writes.

We said that one of the differences between the Cross and the Mass was that in the Mass the sacrifice is offered without bloodshed, whereas on the Cross there were the heart-rending scenes of Crucifixion. A second difference is that on the Cross Our Lord was alone while in the Mass we are with Him. How we are with Him, will be made clear if we examine the Offertory, the Consecration and the Communion.

OFFERTORY

In order to apply the merits of redemption to our souls we must recapitulate in ourselves the death to sin which was brought about on the Cross. Hence, the first act is the offering of ourselves in union with Christ. In the early Church this was done by offering the very same elements which Our Lord Himself offered at the Last Supper; namely, bread and wine. In the early Church the faithful brought bread and wine to the Mass and some of each was used by the priest for the sacrifice. There are some intrinsic reasons why these elements should have been used, even apart from their Divine authorization. First, bread and wine had been the traditional nourishment of most men through history. Bread, as it were, is the very marrow of the earth and wine is as its very blood. The faithful, therefore, in offering that which has given them their physical sustenance and life, are equivalently giving themselves. A second reason is that no two substances in nature better represent unity than do bread and wine. Bread is made from a multiplicity of grains of wheat, wine from a multiplicity of grapes. So the faithful, who are many, combine to make one offering with Christ. A third reason is that few elements in nature better symbolize sacrifice than wheat and grapes. Wheat does not become bread until it has passed through the Calvary of a winter and has been subjected to the tortures of the mill. Grapes do not become wine until they have trodden the Gethsemane of the wine press. Today, the faithful no longer bring bread and wine to the Sacrifice of the Mass but they bring the equivalent; that is the reason why the collection is often taken up at what is called the Offertory of the Mass. The material sacrifice which they make for the Mass is still a symbol of their spiritual incorporation in the death of Christ. Though they bring no bread and wine, they bring that which buys bread and wine, and these elements still represent the material of their united sacrifice.

CONSECRATION

We have offered ourselves to God as Our Lord offered Himself to His Heavenly Father. The essence of Christianity is the reproduction of what happened to Our Blessed Lord in the life of every single person in the world. The human nature which He took was the pattern, or model nature, for all of us. As He was crucified, rose again and ascended into glory for the redemption of the world, so every person is to offer his human nature freely to Our Blessed Lord and to die to sin in order to live in grace and glory with Him. The Mass represents the peak of that incorporation into the death and glory of Christ. In the Offertory we present ourselves to God under the form of bread and wine.

Now we come to the Consecration, when what is known as Transubstantiation takes place. We are beginning to die to the lower part of ourselves in order to live to Christ. Transubstantiation means that when the words of Consecration are pronounced, the substance of the bread becomes the substance of the Body of Christ, and the substance of the wine becomes the substance of His Blood. It has for its effect a new presence without bloodshed, of the offering of Calvary. In the Mass, there is not another offering, but only another presence of the same offering through the ministry of the priest.

The bread and wine are not consecrated together but separately. First the bread which becomes His Body, then the wine which becomes His Blood. This separate consecration of the bread and wine is a kind of mystical separation of His Body and His Blood, equivalent to the way He died on Calvary.

The consecration of the Mass does not mean that Our Lord dies again, for He never can die again in His own individual human nature, which is now in glory at the right hand of the Father. But He prolongs His death in us. That is one of the reasons that there must always be a servant or server, a member of the Church in attendance when the Mass is said. The Mass is the offering of the living Church and its faithful. It is almost as if at the moment of consecration Our Lord were saying: "I cannot die again in My human nature which is in glory at the right hand of the Father, but Peter, Paul, Mary, James, Ann: you give Me your human nature and I will die again in you." In the Offertory we presented ourselves for sacrifice with Christ; in the Consecration we die with Him. We apply His death to ourselves that we may share His glory. The eternal now breaks in upon the temporal and there is nothing more solemn on the face of the earth than the awe-inspiring moment of consecration. It is not a prayer, it is not a hymn, it is not something said, it is a Divine act which enables us to apply the Cross to ourselves.

Though primarily the words of consecration mean that the Body and Blood of Christ is present on the altar, there is a secondary meaning which concerns ourselves. The priests and the people are also called to make such a total dedication of themselves, by death to sin and lower life, that they can say: "This is my body, this is my blood. I care not if the species or the accidents or the appearances of my life remain, such as my duty in life, my avocations, my employment. Let all these things stay as they are, but what I am before Thee, my intellect, my will, my body, my soul, let all these be so changed that I may be not mine but Thine." Then we realize in the deepest sense, the words of St. Paul to the Galatians: "With Christ I hang upon the cross." We might put it into a prayer, saying: "I give myself to God, here is my body, take it. Here is my blood, take it. Here is my soul, my will, my energy, my strength, my property, my wealth—all that I have. It is Yours. Take it! Consecrate it! Offer it! Offer it with Thyself to the Heavenly Father in order that He, looking down on this great sacrifice, may see only Thee, His Beloved Son, in Whom He is well pleased. Transmute the poor bread of my life into Thy Divine Life; charge the wine of my wasted life with Thy Divine Spirit; unite my broken heart with Thy Heart; change my cross into a crucifix. Let not my abandonment, my sorrow and my bereavement go to waste. Gather up the fragments, and as the drop of water is absorbed by the wine at the Offertory of the Mass, let my life be absorbed in Thine; let my little cross be entwined with Thy great Cross so that I may purchase the joys of everlasting happiness in union with Thee."

THE COMMUNION

In the Offertory, we are like lambs being led to the slaughter. In the Consecration, we are the lambs who are slaughtered in the lower part of our sinful selves. In the Communion, we find that we have not died at all but that we have come to life.

In order to understand by opposites what takes place in Holy Communion, consider the nature of a totalitarianism such as Communism. In such a philosophy of life, every person must surrender himself totally and completely, body and soul, mind and will, action and life, to a human dictator. In Christianity there is also a total surrender; we give ourselves completely and entirely to God through His Divine Son, Jesus Christ.

But here comes the great difference. In Communism those who deliver themselves over to the state are surrendering to materialism, for they are denying God and the soul. When one gives oneself up to that which is material, one becomes possessed by it, as a drowning man becomes possessed by the materiality of water, and a burning man becomes possessed by the materiality of fire, and a suffocated man becomes possessed by the materiality of earth. Communism can never enrich or exalt the souls of its followers.

But when there is a dedication to God, and when our death is to the lower part of ourselves as it is in the Consecration of the Mass, then we get back our souls ennobled and enriched. We begin at last to be free, glorified, divinized, exalted. We find that, after all, our death was no more permanent in the Consecration than was the death of Christ on Calvary, for in Holy Communion we surrender our humanity and we receive Divinity. We give up time and we get eternity, we give up our sin and we receive grace, we surrender our self-will and receive the omnipotence of Divine will. We give up petty loves and receive the Flame of Love, we give up our nothingness and we receive all. For Christ has said: "He . . . who loses his life for my sake . . . will save it."

There is another life above the life of the body; namely, the life of the soul. Just as the life of the body is the soul so, too, the life of the soul is God. This Divine life we receive in Communion. If the sunlight and moisture and the chemicals of the earth could speak they would say to the plants: "Unless you eat me you shall not have life in you;" if the plants and the herbs of the field could speak, they would say to the animals: "Unless you eat me you shall not have life in you;" if the animals and the plants and the chemicals of the universe could speak they would say to man: "Unless you eat me you shall not have life in you." So, too, the Son of God says to us that unless we receive of Him we shall not have Divine life in us. The law of transformation holds sway, the lower is transformed into the higher; chemicals into plants, plants into animals, animals into man and man into God without, however, man ever losing his personal identity. Hence the word that is used for Communion is "to receive" Our Lord, for literally we do receive the Divine life, more significantly than a babe receives human life as it is nursed by the mother, for in this latter case, the human is being nourished by the human, but in Communion the human receives Divine life from God. But like all words, even this one has some imperfection, for in communion it is not so much we who receive Christ as Christ who receives us, incorporating us into Himself.

We know we do not deserve this. All love really feels itself unworthy. The lover is always on his knees, the beloved always on a pedestal. Hence before receiving Communion we repeat with the priest: "*Domine non sum dignus*"—O, Lord, I am not worthy. It is as if we were holding ourselves back, conscious of the fact that we are unworthy of the Divine gift.

It is to be noted that there is no such thing as Communion without a sacrifice. Just as we cannot have the natural communion of eating, unless vegetables have been torn up from their roots and subjected to fire, and animals have been subjected to the knife and slain, and then submitted to purgation, so neither can we have Communion with Christ unless there is first a death. That is why the Mass is not just a Communion service; it is a sacrifice which ends in Communion. Communion is the consequence of Calvary; we live by what we slay. Our bodies live by the slaying of the beasts of the field and the plants of the garden; we draw life from their crucifixion; we slay them not to destroy but to have life more abundantly. We immolate them for the sake of communion.

By a beautiful paradox of Divine love, God makes His Cross the very means of our salvation and our life. We have slain Him; we have nailed Him there and crucified Him; but the Love in His eternal Heart could not be extinguished. He *willed* to give us the very life we slew; to give us the very Food we destroyed; to nourish us with the very Bread we buried, and the very Blood we poured forth. He made our very crime into a happy fault; He turned a Crucifixion into a Redemption; a Consecration into a Communion; a death into Life Everlasting.

And it is just this that makes man all the more mysterious! Why man should be loved, is no mystery. But why he does not love in return, is a great mystery. Why should Our Lord be the Great Unloved; why should Love not be loved? He is loved in all who unite themselves with Christ the Priest and the Victim.

It is this drama of Redemption that M. Daniel-Rops has sought to clarify in this magnificent book in which he unites his profound knowledge of Christian tradition with the literary talents that have brought him the high honor of membership in the French Academy. M. Daniel-Rops' words have been complemented by the photographs of Mr. Yousuf Karsh, who has taken the mechanics out of photography and made it a fine art. The chapel which appears in the photographs is our own private chapel and the altar boy is our nephew, Francis Jerome Cunningham III. Literary and liturgical assistance of an invaluable kind was supplied by the Very Rev. Msgr. Edward T. O'Meara, S.T.D., the Assistant National Director of The Society for the Propagation of the Faith. And the translation from the French by Mr. Alastair Guinan, as well as his useful notes, has preserved the full flavor of the original.

MOST REVEREND FULTON J. SHEEN, D.D., Ph.D.

Preface

EVERY DAY, wherever the Cross has been set up, Mass is said . . . In villages and in teeming cities, there is the Mass; in the Far North or in some tropical hut, there is the Mass, as well. In the early hours of morn, in some lonely church dotted here and there with a few worshippers, Mass is said by a priest who seems to be functioning for the sake of a mere handful of the devout; and, with high pomp, amid a vast multitude gathered in the brilliantly lighted Basilica of St. Peter, Mass is said after the Vicar of Christ has been borne on the *Sedia Gestatoria* before the Altar to the sound of joyous acclamation. Times unnumbered, and at every moment of the day, Mass is said in one or another place throughout the world. His Holiness Pius XII, in his Encyclical "Mediator Dei," calls the Mass "the chief act of divine worship, the apex and the core of the Christian religion."

Yet what does this act mean to us who assist at the culmination of the worship man wishes to offer to God, to us who through it come face to face with the essence and the core of our faith, to us who attend Mass; and what does it make of us? A young man of our day who was seeking for something in which he might believe, cried out: "These people come down from Golgotha, and then they talk about the weather!" It is to a great act of immolation that we have been called, to the commemoration of an act of sacrifice which is all the more unexampled in that the victim is at once willing to suffer and nevertheless wholly innocent of wrong-doing. We are here confronted with the unfathomed mystery of the ransoming blood of that spotless victim of sin, in whose weakness is perfect strength and in whose life death dies. Were it not that thoughtlessness and heedless familiarity lie over our souls like a hard crust, we could not bear to come to Mass as though it were but some conventionalism of social ceremony; for we would realize that it should mean everything to us, and that in face of it providing Love's answer to Faith's most tantalizing and contradictory problems, we might well feel our minds struck dumb, our sensibilities deeply touched, and our hearts themselves wholly subdued by love.

The meaningful core of the Mass lies in this, that it is *par excellence* a drama which is ceaselessly enacted before us, a tragedy everlastingly prolonged. The name by which this drama has been known since the sixth century is a term taken from the formulary with which, aforetime, it was brought to its closure—the formulary, *Ite Missa est*—and it seems all too curt a word wherewith to clothe so ineffable a mystery. It seems, indeed, that other names for the Mass which were once in use, are more suitable—Thanksgiving; Liturgy; the Breaking of Bread; Synaxis, or assembly; or, to follow the usage of Tertullian, Justin Martyr, and St. Cyprian of Carthage, we might call it *Dominica Passio*, the Passion of the Lord. Herein lies the truth, for it is the Passion of Christ which inspires the Mass, that Passion besought, declared, manifested, and fulfilled. Everything in the Mass converges on this fundamental fact of Christian faith, that our Redemption was wrought by the sacrifice of the Cross; and it is in relation to it rather than to a simple formulary of dismissal that the Mass is best understood.

At first the Mass preserved, in precise terms, the memory of that Last Supper at which Jesus, but a short time before He suffered and died, blessed the bread and the wine and made of them His body and His blood, and then said: "Do this for a commemoration of me" (Lk. 22:19). His pregnant words, effecting by transubstantiation the change of two very ordinary earthly substances into supernatural substances, are the vehicles of a two-fold message. By them was foretold the death of Christ in willing offering of Himself, even before the enemies of Jesus became the ministrants at His oblation: "So", says St. Paul, "so it is the Lord's death that you are heralding, whenever you eat this bread, and drink this cup, until he comes" (I Cor. 11:26). And, by the same token, inasmuch as He offered to His disciples the bread and the wine which had been so marvelously changed, He made them sharers at another Table as well as at that Last Supper; that is to say, at the Table of everlasting life. Therefore, the Mass is a remembrance of three truths: it is the re-enactment of the words and gestures which marked the consecration that took place at the Last Supper; it is the lively memorial, charged with its own dramatic meaning, of the sacrifice offered on Calvary's hill; it is the banquet-table to which all the baptized are called.

Historically, the kernel of the Mass lies in its being a presentment of the Last Supper through the repetition of those words and acts there taught us by Christ, words and acts whose fathomless significance the faith of the first Christians knew how to apprehend. So it is that there may be pictured those early Masses which the Apostles celebrated after the Ascension Day or after the first Pentecost. They were quite simple, and indeed they consisted of no more than the careful repetition of what the Apostles had been taught. This note of an austere simplicity endured throughout the whole apostolic age. Do we not see St. Paul, while on one of his missionary journeys, officiating at "the breaking of bread" in a simple room on the third floor of a dwelling house while surrounded by a group which the little room could scarcely contain? (Acts 20:7 sqq). This sacred Supper was not separated from the Agapé or Love Feast in which the primitive Christians gathered together that they might bind themselves to fellowship in the Lord.

After the passing of almost twenty centuries, the Mass has lost the note of stark austerity. Other elements have been superimposed on the fundamental evangelical structure. The chief of these are a direct inheritance from the divine service of the older dispensation. Were not the Apostles children of Moses? Were they not convinced that they were showing their fidelity to the precepts of his law when they gave adhesion to the Revelation of Christ? As the Gospels and the Book of the Acts testify, divine service in the Jewish synagogues was made up of two parts. The *prayer service* comprised the singing or recitation of prayers from the Scriptures, especially from one or another of those wonderful passages in the Book of Psalms wherein human fervency pours itself out in a fashion elsewhere unsurpassed. The *didactic service* consisted in listening to readers who took up the holy books of the Law and the Prophets. These characteristic notes were maintained in Christian services of worship; and even when Christians had entirely discontinued participation in the Jewish worship, they retained its chief features in their own. In this lies the root of the prayers at the beginning of Mass and of the readings from the Epistles and the Gospels.

The Mass became set much as we now know it, insofar as concerns its broad structure, at about the close of the third century. Although this or that part may show some growth or some diminution in importance from the usages of that time, the general plan of the ceremony is even now just such as it was then. However, in primitive times the details of the Mass were not as rigorously fixed as they are in our day, and apart from an adherence to basic matters, there was a degree of permissible latitude which allowed the bishop, or even the celebrating priest, to express himself in extemporaneous prayer. Notable divergencies in the manner of celebrating Mass long flourished, as can easily be seen by taking up and comparing some of the old *Sacramentaries*, those Missals so magnificently written and painted which were in use at solemn ceremonials during the whole period of the high Middle Ages. Even in our own time, one may find certain differences in Rite or Use attached, by privilege, to particular dioceses (Lyon and Milan are two examples) or to religious orders (as the Carthusians, Dominicans, or Premonstratensians). Above all is this distinction to be perceived in the sumptuous and prolix Liturgies of the East when these are contrasted with the relatively simple Rites of the West in our day.

During the course of the centuries, certain new elements have been received into the Mass according to the living tradition of the Church; and just as the more elaborate music which succeeded the graver measures of the old plainchant clearly gives evidence of freedom from the restraints imposed on the more primitive constituents of the old liturgy, all these newer elements possess in common two characteristics: they interrupt the course of the eucharistic prayer, and they often display great subjectivity and individualism. The *Gloria*, for example, was originally an acclamatory hymn proper to the Midnight Mass of Christmas when it gave voice to the joy of Christian hearts in commemorating the Redeemer's birth; while the *Credo*, to cite another instance, is an individualistic proclamation of personal faith and belief which found a place in the Mass at about the year 1000, being then most probably introduced to repel heretical doubt. Certain acts which to us would appear to be of manifest necessity in the Mass, such as the *Great Elevation*, are likewise later additions to its primitive structure. In this instance, the solemn showing of the Host to the people serves as a reply to the separatist's contention that God is not present in the Eucharistic Elements. There is something attractively persuasive in the traditional adornments thus added to the framework of the Mass: they prove, indeed, the living heritage of a faith which ceaselessly re-states itself.

The Mass in its present rigidly regulated form, as we now know it in the West, was fixed on the morrow of the Council of Trent by St. Pius V. By his Bull, "Quo primum" of 1570, he expressed a wish to recall the Mass to its antique norms; he attempted at once to disencumber it of certain incidental elements and to impose its observance in uniform fashion throughout Latin Christendom. The Mass was thus given definitive form by being closely associated with the Primacy of the Apostolic See and the authority of St. Peter's successor, while the Mass Book endorsed by the Tridentine Fathers was none other than that used in the Eternal City, the *Roman Missal*.

Therefore was it declared in the Catechism of the Council of Trent that no part of that Missal ought be considered *vain or superfluous;* that not even the least of its phrases is to be thought wanting or insignificant. The shortest of its formularies, phrases even which take no more than a few seconds to pronounce, form integral parts of a whole wherein are drawn together and set forth God's gift, Christ's sacrifice, and the grace which is dowered upon us. This whole conception has in view a sort of spiritual symphony in which all themes are taken as being expressed, developed, and unified under the guidance of one purpose.

What then is the plan of the Mass? Its traditional division into the Mass of the Catechumens and the Mass of the Faithful is the result of historical circumstances; for the first part owes its existence to a provision for admitting to the common worship of Christians the unbaptized neophytes as well as the baptized, while the Mass of the Faithful is so called because after a certain point in the service had been reached, the unbaptized were, in olden days, dismissed. But it is the very manner of development assumed by the liturgy, it is the arc of its fulfillment, which best marks out the moments or "acts" of the Mass in the very sense in which that term is used in respect of the drama. There are five such acts. In the first of them when I am on the threshold of this sacramental action, I *pray:* I beg that God will forgive what I have done amiss; I speak to Him of my will to know Him; I raise my voice in praise and in supplication. In the second, I *hear* the teaching of the Church, first as that teaching has been received from the Apostles or was prophetically declared in the inspired books of the Old Law, and later in the words of Jesus Himself in the Gospel. The substance of this teaching is summed up in the *Credo* which I then repeat by way of affirming my assent to it. Next, I find myself entering upon the sacrificial liturgy properly so considered. Christ Himself offers Himself in an oblation which is the sacramental core of the Mass, and it is my privilege to join in this grace-giving act. I therefore *offer,* through the ministration of the priestly celebrant who is at once my witness and my representative, I *offer* those fruits of the earth which are to be changed; and this offering is, in itself, symbolic of that more personal, and wholly interior oblation, which I make of myself, so that offering and offerer become one. The fourth division is the most profound in meaning: it comprises the *sacrificial act* itself by which and in which the victim is immolated. It is I myself who by intimate participation in the sacrificial action of the priest, it is I myself who effect this immolation in which the victim of the *sacrifice* and its ministrant are one: again the divine Body is nailed to the Cross; again the redeeming Blood gushes forth. And, finally, in obedience to the will of Christ, I *receive* the Holy Communion and am nourished at the Table of everlasting life.

So it is that, step by step, the liturgy of the Mass unfolds itself before our eyes in an impressive harmony which allows of no comparison. In it and by it is every aspect of man's religion duly accomplished: the Mass is the summation and complement of all man's hopes and good purposes. The Mass is the implementation of an interchange between God and myself: by it all that I would seek in my prayer is gradually brought to fulfillment almost before I have put my desire into words. Yet it may be asked if its effect is something which concerns nothing more than the relations existing between God and myself? It is true, indeed, that by the first of the new commandments we are enjoined to love God with our whole mind and heart; but it must not be overlooked that the second which is, as we have been taught, *like unto the first,* requires that man love his neighbor as himself. He has not understood the Mass at all who has failed to perceive that by it these two commandments are unceasingly recalled to our remembrance.

The Mass first came into being as an act of common prayer: it was the prayer of the re-united Twelve, the prayer of those early Christian believers who were so bound in devotion one to another that they shared their goods in common, it was the prayer of the Martyrs who mingled their blood in a common confession of the One Lord. It is no more than the simple truth to declare that at Mass we are all but little cells in one body, each of us a sheep that belongs to the one fold. The most outstandingly beautiful prayers of the liturgy—and they are among the most ancient as well—the *Collects,* the *Secrets,* and the *Postcommunions,* are not grasped in their true significance unless they be considered as expressing *the common prayer.* They teach a lesson which is re-stated by the *Mementos*—one of the living, the other of the dead— which we find inserted in the prayer of the Consecration itself: beyond all claims of time and space, beyond the all-compelling exactions of death itself, we make ourselves ready for union with God in just the degree that we are joined in fellowship one with another; and this is the whole sense and burden of the Communion of Saints.

For the Mass is born of a two-fold meaning and purpose. It is my own most urgent concern: herein lie my life and my death. It is for me, all unworthy as I am, it is for me that every Mass is celebrated: *"for you* it is that there gushes forth this drop of My Blood . . ."* Yet, the fullest meaning of the Mass is unrealized unless it be shared in fellowship by me with all the children of God, unless they somehow join me in the path that leads to the Light, for *the soul when lifted up, shall draw the world unto it;* and each one of us is charged with the welfare of all. It is, of course, only the whole Church, considered from its very beginnings as extending and enduring until the end of time, that is worthy and able to gather the elements and to set forth the oblation in this sacrifice to the Infinite God. The Mass is our own concern: it concerns every one of us. And it is as one individual, however insignificant, in the great multitude of human souls for whom Christ thirsted and whom He has redeemed in His own Blood, it is as one individual united to all my fellows by faith and in hope, that I now will to assist at Mass the while my heart is bowed in love and in expectation of the coming of the Lord.

This is the Mass

I

Introïbo ad Altare Dei

THE PRAYERS AT THE FOOT OF THE ALTAR

We stand on the threshold of the Mass: *introibo*, I will go unto the altar of God. These are prayers of preparation. Nowadays, they are said by the priest at the foot of the altar steps; formerly, he began them while leaving the sacristy, as a personal act of approach to the holy mysteries; and there is a certain tone about them even yet which befits private prayer. Historically, they represent a late addition to the Mass. Their first appearance dates only from the seventh century, and they did not come into general usage until 1570 when Pius V made the Roman Missal obligatory. The words of these prayers are meaningful, and Psalm 42 recalls the exiled Jews grieving by the waters of Babylon. They wept for their despoiled altar, for their abandoned Holy Place. But these words testify, too, to a faith which stands unshaken, to an entire trust in God. As the verses of this psalm succeed each other, it is hope that out-rings sorrow. For this reason, in the early Church—at Milan, for example, in the days of St. Ambrose—the newly baptized sang this psalm on Easter Eve, when they were first admitted to a full share in the whole Mass. "I will go up to the Altar of God, the giver of triumphant happiness." How apparent and how meaningful do these words of Scripture become as we think of them in the light of a re-birth, of a restoration, of youthful fervor; for it is with a youthful heart, in a spirit overflowing with joy, that we should come before the living God.

I AM COME, my Lord, in a ready spirit, armed with hope and with love. I look on this Mass as a happy oasis in my life, as a source of refreshment and of vigor, so that with a right heart I may resume my work; so that the burdens which, oft-times, I find beyond bearing may be lightened through Your loving kindness and Your indulgent aid.

How many are the hours I spend without a thought of You, my God; forgetful even of my own soul, but in the grip of alien forces! Keep me mindful of You, and of what I am to You: for to think of one is to think of the other. I pray that these moments which are made holy by being passed in Your Presence, may be a source of faith, of fervor, and of joy.

Take away from me this bitterness which throttles me, this harsh and agonizing dryness which holds me in its grip, this darksome discouragement which broods around me. Cleanse me from secret leanings to sin, from inclinations impelling me to choose what is unworthy, from all the evil that I would not and that I yet do. At the very beginning of this Mass, make me ready to be what You would have me be.

My trust in You is boundless, and my very first word is one of entire confidence in You. I believe in You; in You do I place my trust: it is You alone who are the rock of my being and the fulcrum of my strength. And it is because I am no more in Your sight than a reed, a reed which rests in Your hands, that I know myself to be strong.

Therefore am I glad, glad in my Lord. There awaits me a renewal of my forces, in which my soul shall come to full growth. By the glad light of this confrontation with You for which I now make ready, my Lord, I beg You to lead me henceforth along the way in which I should go. Guide me by Truth, which is the right hand of Your Love.

II

Confiteor

THE GENERAL CONFESSION OF SINS

In the very instant of its surrender to joy, the soul is held back by a heaviness within itself, as a wall of separation looms between the soul and God. This vexing obstacle is the soul's knowledge of its own sinfulness. In the primitive Church, which had its roots in the heart of Christ, there was a spontaneous sense of the soul's need to ask for pardon at the beginning of Mass. (And, indeed, it seems that there may have then existed a penitential rite like the washing of the disciples' feet by Jesus before the Last Supper.) Little by little, there came into usage the formal declaration of the soul's sinful state and an accompanying plea for pardon. In the eighth and ninth centuries, under the title of *Apologia*, devout souls began to compose *excusatory prayers* in which pleading mingled with confession. The Roman Missal as drawn up in 1570 preserves one of these formularies constructed in the dramatic manner associated with the four stages of a trial: the soul appears before the bar of justice, the soul confesses its guilt, the advocates plead, and pardon is granted. This is a public collective prayer in which priest and people antiphonally acknowledge their sinfulness, not just privately, but in the face of the whole Church, of all her saintly witnesses, and even in the face of the very powers of Heaven.

Thus does the *Confiteor* strike, initially, that note of the sense of fellowship, of communion one with another, which marks Mass-goers. The thrice repeated act of deep repentance, at *mea culpa,* when the hand strikes the breast in an old biblical and monastic gesture, brings consolation to the sinner in his racking sorrow; for is it not written that the prayer of the humble shall be heard before the Most High? (Ecclus. 35:21).

ALL HEAVEN is listening, all the great saints of the past: I am in the presence not alone of Him before whose gaze nothing lies hid, not alone of that strange and penetrating discernment which belongs to God's angels, but as well in the sight of every man and woman strong enough to have lived by love, of every saint and martyr whose mere existence is a condemnation of my own sinfulness.

What shall I, a sinner, now be saying as against me rises the voice of the accuser, the voice that brings me sharply to account? The knowledge that I am guilty suffices to stop my own voice; it forbids my attempt at any defence.

Against me stand my own actions which, even though human justice might not deem them worthy of reproof, I know to be in some sense wanting or even worse. My secret thoughts rise up from those shoals of wretchedness and dejection which the self-satisfied sloth of human complacency serves but to conceal. And I am faced, too, with all that I have left undone, with my failures, with my back-slidings and strayings, with all the overwhelming burden of my unspoken assents to wrong.

I would that the thrice-repeated gesture of penitence, made upon my breast, might bestir my heart and awaken my soul from the torpor of its heavy sleep, by recalling me to all that I should do.

Now all around me are also the mysterious forces of loving kindness. All these saints of past times, all the powers of Heaven, serving as a tribunal of accusation and judgment, are become my intercessors before the Infinite One. The Virgin's purity, the martyrs' blood, the shining forbearance of the saints, are become my safeguard in the mysterious economy of the sharing of merit through the Communion of Saints.

And while the words of absolution resound, I cast aside thought of my fear that I shall fall again tomorrow and have to start over once more, and I stand upright in joy regained as, suddenly, I sense an indescribable relief.

III

The Kissing of the Altar

THE PRIEST GOES UP TO THE HOLY TABLE

The prayers at the foot of the altar were but an introduction; the priest now goes up, step by step, to the altar. Using some words from that Psalm (84: *Benedixisti Domine*) which is so associated with the joys of Christmastide, he has first prayed that God would show His face to His people in order that in Him they may find their joy. But at the very moment of his beginning to go up the steps a shadow falls over the heart of the priest and, in the words of an old prayer which was already in use in Rome in the fifth century (*Aufer a nobis, quaesumus, Domine, iniquitates nostras . . .*), he implores the Lord to cleanse the soul desirous of penetrating to the holy place.

Now the priest stands before the altar, before the most holy object which the church contains, before that altar which is its center and its apex, an object of a mysterious meaningfulness which can never be fully fathomed. A symbol of Christ, is not the altar also the place which serves to table the Body and Blood of the Crucified? And is it not also, as St. Ambrose tells us, the very type of

that holy Body itself, for on the day the altar was consecrated it received the unction proper to the Lord's Anointed when it was annealed with the Sacred Chrism? The five crosses which are cut into the stone recall Our Lord's five wounds. The altar also represents the Church: the relics of her saints are encased within the table, and the priest who is come to celebrate the Sacrifice does so in the Church's name. In the presence of the awesome sense of glory which emanates from the altar, the priest, in devout veneration, touches that holy table with his lips. Now by this kiss he signifies the union typified by the kiss which the Spouse gives to His Bride. And indeed, what the priest is proposing to accomplish here is nothing other than to forge the union of the Church to her Master, of the soul to its Redeemer. It is this same excess of joy which causes the priest thus to salute the altar that we feel rising up within us in our moments of deepest inspiration. Then it is that we dress that altar of our souls, that altar whereon Christ desires to rest.

AS YOUR ALTAR, my Lord, stands in the very heart of this church, visible to all by being set in that highest place where spiritual truth rises to fitting eminence, grant that, in my own heart, concern for You may take the highest place in the very core and apex of my being.

As this tabernacle shelters Your living presence which with fullest faith I now confess, grant that my soul may learn to know You, whom no man calls to account; and that you may become nearer to me than is my innermost thought.

As in this holy table are enclosed the memorials of a cloud of witnesses, the holy relics of Your saints, our pledges of everlasting life, grant that I may fully appreciate my place in Your Church, and that my soul may cleave to You in the Church.

As the priest now devoutly bows before Your altar, awed by its sacramental glory, grant me to know my own littleness and Your greatness; grant me so to subdue and trample under earthly pride that I may seek and find fulfillment, not in my own poor vanity, but in Him who alone endures.

Finally, as this kissing of the altar is an avowal and an earnest of that love before which the delights of all earthly loves languish and pale, grant, Lord Jesus, that I may love You, that I may more fully know You, that I may do only what You will as I bow before the secret altar which is set within my soul.

IV

The Mark of the Beginning

THE SIGN OF THE CROSS

The celebrant goes to the right side of the altar and, from the book which he finds there, he reads a short prayer. This is the *Introït* or Entrance Versicle—the *Ingressa* (or going-in verse), as it is called in the Ambrosian Liturgy. Its meaning becomes clear only in the light of an understanding of the old ceremonial of which these few words are the only surviving memorial. In the early days of the Roman Church, the Pope went from the Lateran Palace in a solemn cortege of his attendant clergy, deacons, and acolytes, to the particular sanctuary in which Mass was, that day, to be said. This rite existed in the fifth century under St. Celestine V, and it was later embellished and amplified by St. Gregory the Great. In it lies the origin of the processional entrance. Psalms were chanted by alternating choirs—in antiphonal style, as it is called—psalms which were specially chosen for their consonance with the underlying intention of the particular day's sacrifice. Thus they were joyous in Advent, but mournful in Lent. On saints' days they

hymned their glorious triumph, and when the Epiphany and the Transfiguration were being commemorated their theme was the royalty of Christ. Thus the *Introït* became an entrance-song or introduction in a two-fold sense. In our time, there is but a vestige of this impressive rite in the use of a single anthem followed by a psalm verse (or, on occasion, of a passage from some other book of Scripture), with *Gloria Patri* and the repetition of the anthem. Nevertheless, even this foreshortened, elliptical *Introït* keeps its function, differing as it does from day to day and serving always as a sort of spiritual introduction which, by a few brief words, states the theme or point of emphasis of the Mass formulary which it opens. As he says the words of the *Introït*, the celebrant makes that holy sign which is, above all others, the mark of the beginning; in it and by it are all things done and brought to fulfillment: it is the emblem which sums up the fullness of all things known and concealed, the sacred sign of the Cross.

IN THE NAME of the Father, and of the Son, and of the Holy Ghost. My Lord, grant that I may now make this accustomed gesture as though I were doing it for the first time; grant that what I know so well as oft-times to do rather ill, I may now so make as to feel the full joy of its meaning while I sense, as it were for the first time, the power of the Cross.

At the beginning of Mass, as I approach Your sacrifice, let the Cross by which I am ransomed be rooted in my heart. Through it may my life and my sufferings be united to Your humanity and to the sufferings and to the sorrow which You accepted. May the death which I fearfully await be joined with that sacrificial death which You willed to meet and to undergo in Love.

Grant, my Lord, that through this sign which evokes the sanctifying power of the Name Ineffable, all my hopes and purposes may be guided by the Three Persons whose name I now invoke; that in the grace of the Son I may be strengthened and guided on my path to the Father; that I may come to Him in the truth and by the flame of the Holy Spirit.

In the name of the Father, and of the Son, and of the Holy Ghost. My Lord, as my hand passes from my forehead to my breast, and from shoulder to shoulder, may this holy sign dominate all my thoughts and become the mainstay of my being, so that despite all my sinfulness, despite all that wretchedness of my heart which to You alone lies open, I may yet know myself to be blessed by You, healed by You, marked with Your own seal.

V

The Mercy and the Glory of God

THE KYRIE AND THE GLORIA

There are two notions which, like musical themes in a symphony, recur again and again in the Mass: we here find them brought together in two prayers which are complementary each to the other, the *Kyrie* and the *Gloria*. To give glory to God and to beg His mercy are the two purposes which link man to God: it is because we know that God is Almighty that we beseech Him to have mercy upon us. And are not all the varying nuances of these inseparable purposes expressed in that beautiful gesture by which the priest first extends and elevates, and then rejoins, his hands? It is a gesture which sums up all our yearning for divine things the while, by increasing our fervency, it bespeaks our hope of salvation.

The *Kyrie* is a remnant of those litanic dialogues, of those acclamatory prayers, which rose up spontaneously in the breast of the primitive Church. It originated in the Greek-speaking East, perhaps in Jerusalem where the Spanish pilgrim, Etheria,[1] heard it sung about the year 500; and it is in Greek that we still say it. After the opening of the ceremony by the *Introït* with its three verses from Holy Writ, this simple plea carries, to the Three Divine Persons in turn, our heartfelt need and purposive desire for salvation.

Then, at once, there is intoned a hymn to the Majesty of God. The *Gloria* is a very old prayer, already in existence in the second century, which was incorporated into the Roman Mass in the sixth century.[2] It opens appropriately with the words in which the angels sang praise "to God in the highest;" for is not every Mass a renewal, in some sense, of Christmas, and does it not mark, once more, the Coming of Our Lord? Beginning with this Gospel verse, the ages of faith launch into a hymn of praise which, in its free-flowing fulsomeness, is like a torrent of love unleashed.

Yet even this emphasis on the Father's glory cannot conceal from man his own wretched state.

For this reason, when address is made to Christ our Mediator, the hymn re-echoes the appeal for mercy voiced by the *Kyrie:* it is because He is holy, because He is the Lord, because He is the Most High God, that Jesus brings us salvation.

And it is in suggesting the shining reflection of the bright glory of Father, Son, and Holy Spirit, which is itself the pledge of salvation in a believer's soul, that this most beautiful of hymns is brought to its end in sublime simplicity.

44

NOW THAT, three times, the three-fold petition has been raised to You, and has come from the depths of the souls of all Your creatures throughout all ages as a cry of hope, as a petition for pardon;

Now that the angelic choirs and the unforgotten voices of all our brethren in the Faith have acclaimed Your glory, and have given thanks for the Name of Your glory;

Grant, my Lord, that my healed spirit may be established before You in quietude, so that I may enter even into Your presence and there cry out to You in plain words: "My God, I love You; it is You that I worship; my God, show mercy to me;"—for having said this, I shall have said all.

VI

Made One in the Lord

THE COLLECT

It is not enough to have adored and to have asked for mercy: a sense of unity is part of every Mass. *"Dominus vobiscum,"* cries out the priest—"the Lord be with you"—as with extended arms he turns to face the people. And it would appear that the Liturgy seeks by means of this action, by the employment of this old salutation borrowed from Biblical usage, to satisfy a wish that all the faithful may be gathered together and made one in their supplication. This action is repeated at eight solemn times during the Mass: it is just such a gathering together of suppliants as it bespeaks that inspires the prayers called *Collects* which now follow. They are grave as Latin inscriptions in their terms and seem as if incised upon medals.

This is one of the chief moments of prayer at Mass, the other times being signalized by the *Secret* and the *Postcommunion* prayers. These prayers are addressed to the Trinity in Unity; and, while the people kneel,[1] the priest with hands extended reads them from the book. Should he have to pronounce the name of Jesus, he bows his head to the altar-cross. Is it because these prayers sum up and gather together all the intentions of the day's sacrifice, that they are called *Collects?* Historically that title recalls the old custom of Urban Rome where, about the fourth century, it was the practice for the whole Christian community to come together in one church that they might proceed with solemnity to the sanctuary chosen for the celebration of the day's Mass: in this sense the Collect is the prayer of the *plebs collecta,* the prayer of the assembled people. Were those Christians of the Middle Ages then so much at fault when they pushed this term further, and explained the word as meaning the *common prayer?* As he recites these prayers is not the priest gathering together, as if in one sheaf, all our hopes and all our good purposes as if to offer them to God?[2] And, once more, is not the kiss with which the celebrant again salutes the altar before saying these prayers, is not the kiss a sign of the entire uniting of the assembly in Christ?

48

LORD, it is not for myself alone I now do pray,
   for selfish prayer is scarce a prayer at all;
But for all these, Your people, seen and unseen, for
   those who bear Your blessèd Sign, for these I pray;
Nor do I now forget those others who know You not,
   or who, knowing, have forsaken Your way:
   For all we are one in You.

With all these, then, I join in that appointed invocation
   which Your church does place upon our lips today;
For to each day is given its own singular fashion
   wherewith to praise You and to pray to You;
That praying thus our lasting wish may come to be
   And we may grasp that which alone abides.

From an undivided heart, and in child-like spirit,
   To all these prayers I do myself unite,
As Your church in due humility does now pour out
   in words of plain and forceful sense,
Mankind's fear of oppression, famine, evil deeds,
   and its need of the dew of Your Love.

Thus guided by the saints whom we do now recall,
   Be they close or distant, familiar or scarce known,
I join the age-long cloud of witnesses
   in ranks unbroken and unceasing,
While with these lips You've given me, I frame the Church's prayer
   And strive to reach the foot of Your Eternal Throne.

VII

The Reading in God's Name

THE EPISTLE

The *Amen* which concludes the *Collects* brings to its end the first part of the Ante-Mass. To that act of religion called *prayer,* there now succeeds another act of religion—that of *listening* to the Word. "I have a message . . . from the Lord," we are told by the Bible (Judges 3:20); and it is to each one of us that the Lord's Word is directed.

If we would seek the origin of these readings, we would have to delve into the most ancient of Christian usages, and to go, in fact, even beyond them to practices dear to the heart of devout Israel. The Service of the synagogue knew such readings from the Law and the Prophets.[1] Have we not seen Jesus reading Isaias to his fellow Jews (Luke 4:16, 21), and did not St. Paul, while on his missionary journeys, take part in similar readings? (Cf. Acts 13:14, 16). The early church faithfully preserved this usage: reading from the sacred books bulked large in the primitive liturgies, and it would be surprising to the first Christians were they now to return and hear only the two brief scraps which are left in to-day's Mass, in its Epistle and Gospel.

In older times, first readings from the Old Testament, then some of the Apostolic Letters, and finally a section of the Gospel itself, were read out for the people to hear and think about. It is this three-part division of preparatory readings which even yet lingers on in the venerable service of Good Friday.[2] At first, these readings were neither brief nor formally delimited beforehand, as they were later made; and the reader used to go on uninterruptedly until the bishop saw fit to signal him that he thought enough had been proposed for the instruction of his hearers. It was only with the appearance of the Roman Missal of 1570 that there came into general usage the two previously selected fragments or pericopes, accommodated to the feast being celebrated.

The first passage which is ordinarily read is the *Epistle*. As this name—*epistola*—indicates, it is a passage from a letter. On Sundays this apostolic letter is almost always taken from the writings of the Apostle Paul. On other occasions—on saints' days, on Lenten ferias, and on Ember days—it is generally from the prophetic writings of the Old Testament that instruction is proposed to us in the reading, which is then termed *Lectio* or Lesson from . . . (whatever its source may happen to be). Evidently, in either case the liturgical purpose is the same, for it shows that in the beginning God speaks to us by the agency of intermediaries, by the mouth of men who are His witnesses or confessors, who are inspired by Him to prepare us that we may later receive His own message directly; and for this reason the reading is done in the name of the Lord.

52

AS AT THE WATERS of Babylon the exiles of Israel were spurred to hope by the voice of Your prophets,

as oppressed Israel found in reading and re-reading the books of Your Law the most certain guardian of their fidelity to You,

as, in its beginnings, Your Church learned, from the reading of the Apostolic Letters, of the joy and the love brought us by Our Saviour,

and as, in days of severe trial Your martyrs found in those apostolic words the motive of their self-sacrifice;

grant, my Lord, that these words of Your chosen witnesses may find my soul tilled, fertile, and ready to bear in joy the fruit of faith;

grant that I may be prepared for that Word by which You have spoken to men from the foundation of the world:

for it is of the Voice of Your Word, my Lord, that it is written that it brings loneliness to an end and fills the heart with strength;

it was that Voice which, on one harvest day, cast Your enemy Saul to the ground and, with a single word, won his heart.

VIII

An Interval of Preparation

BETWEEN THE EPISTLE AND THE GOSPEL

Between the *Epistle* and the *Gospel* we find a group of prayers and chants which might readily be taken by the hasty observer to be mere digressions; no more, that is to say, than bypaths leading away from the general plan of the liturgy; but they are actually most meaningful.

The reading is brought to a close by the usual formulary expressive of thanks—*Deo gratias,* "thanks be to God"—words found so often in the Pauline Epistles, and expressing the notion that we offer thanks because God willed the words that we have just heard to be said or written.

It was the custom in the old Israelitish liturgy that the course of the reading or didactic service be broken by the recitation of psalms. This at once avoided the tedium of monotony and made certain a real participation of the congregation in worship. The chants which are found in our Missal for the present interval are a survival of this usage. That it is a very old usage among the Christians themselves is evident from the testimony of Tertullian in the third century. There are three of these chanted formularies. The *Gradual* is ordinarily composed of words which appropriately refer back to the lesson just read; and it was anciently begun by a singer standing on the step (*gradus*) of the lectern. To his versicle, the congregation replied by taking up a refrain. The *Alleluia* is an old Judaic expression of joy, and is of immemorial usage: it recalls the Lord's coming, and so serves to introduce the *Gospel*. The *Tract* takes the place of the *Alleluia* on days of penance or in seasons of sorrow. It was designed for the voices of the great solo singers of the past, to be sung uninterruptedly by them without the intervention of the choir; and being set to solemn and noble music it is redolent of antiquity. To these formularies the liturgists of the Middle Ages added the *Sequence* or *Prose,* a sort of poetic commentary on the feast being celebrated.

The words of the sequence were originally set to that long series of melismatic neumes in which the *Alleluia* seems to prolong itself in bursts of great and continued joy. These *Proses* are most admirable expressions of Christian fervor: our present Missal retains the *Victimae paschali* for Easter Day, the *Lauda Sion* for Corpus Christi, the *Veni sancte Spiritus* for Whitsunday, the *Dies irae* for Requiem Masses, and that most touching of all, the *Stabat Mater,* which Jacopone da Todi wrote in praise of Our Lady in her Compassion. There is no doubt that these are but adjuncts to the primitive liturgy; but who can be blind to the splendor they lend it?

56

Now the book is brought to its privileged place, to the left corner of the altar, on the side as it were of that altar's heart, wherefrom the words of Christ Himself are to resound. Meanwhile, the priest who is about to speak in Christ's name, prepares himself for that awesome task by begging that God will purify his lips as once did He those of Isaias when an angel touched the great prophet's mouth with a burning coal.

Munda cor. Cleanse my heart; for Your burning coal has more to do than just to make pure these my faithless lips, hitherto so ready to mouth words of anger or of folly;

there are also my ears to be made pure, for they have been overwilling to choose the jangling discords of the world above Your Word; they have welcomed the Lie more easily than the Truth;

there are my eyes, so slow to open to the light because of their fondness for the things of darkness;

there is indeed all my being which waits in need of the purifying fire of Your angel; there is my soul, my judgment, my imagination, and my sinful heart which has betrayed You.

Munda cor. Cleanse my heart; may all my taints and stains be burnt away, and with them all that I know to be foul in me, all that is darksome and hateful to You.

Grant that Your Word may stir in me unfailing faithfulness, rousing me to the love that turns not back but ever moves forward into Your marvelous glad Light.

IX

The Word of God

THE GOSPEL

We are now come to the climax of the Ante-Mass. Up to this point, we have heard the divine message from the lips of men: it is now God Himself who speaks to us! Christ comes to teach us by the example of His life and by His own words.

And it is for this reason that from the very early days of the primitive church, this reading of the *Gospel* has been considered an essential element in the liturgy: in the catacombs it was already something that no one ever thought of dispensing with. This high point in the preparation for the Sacrifice emphasizes the fact that the Christ who came to undergo death for the salvation of each and every one of us is the self-same who teaches each and every one of us what to believe and what to do.

Therefore it is that this point in the Mass is marked and surrounded by an especial degree of solemnity. Is not the Gospel Book another symbol of the Master? Is it not the book which St. John Chrysostom said he could never open without a feeling of awe? At chanted Masses, incense and lights, and at low Masses, the significant gestures of the priest in placing his hand upon the book and in kissing it and marking it with the Cross, express the spirit of veneration due this book.

Having signed themselves with the Cross upon their foreheads, their lips, and their breasts, the congregation listen to the reading of the Gospel while they stand respectfully attentive. The signing of themselves triply with the Cross is to indicate their intellectual acceptance of Truth, their readiness to confess it, and their heartfelt attachment to it.

Ever since the sixth century there has become more and more widespread the present custom of selecting in advance a pericope from one or another of the Four Gospels; and the determining idea in this selection has been to offer an embodiment of the particular lesson which the day's Mass is to reveal to us.

All the other parts of the proper Mass formularies are in dependence, more or less marked, to the Gospel pericope: they serve either as commentaries in respect to what has been declared by it, or as assurances in respect to the fulfillment of that declaration.

This, then, is a point of culmination. It is the very voice of the Incarnate God Himself to which we now listen. And when the reading of His Word is brought to an end, and the voice of our own faith has been raised to acclaim Christ our Master and our Teacher, the whole purpose of the sermon which follows lies, in principle at least, in nothing other than an attempt to develop, to explain, to comment upon the Master's words, that in those words our minds may find enlightenment and our hearts enrichment.

CHRIST SPEAKS TO YOU: hear Him! In these words are the tidings of His life and of His teachings; and they are one.

He is the Child conceived of the Holy Ghost in a Virgin's womb,

He is the new-born Babe in the manger, destined for lowliness and obscurity,

He is the son of a workman, and is Himself a workman, one who knew how to handle the carpenter's tools;

it is He who spoke from the Galilean hills and by the shores of the Lake of Tiberius,

it is He who healed the Centurion's servant, who becalmed the tempest and called Lazarus back to mortal life;

He it is who is man's exemplar, the model of perfection, the pattern none can surpass:

all this is here; listen as He speaks!

It is He who teaches men to love one another,

to pardon enemies and to receive them as brethren,

to be pure as He was, and to be meek and lowly of heart, as well;

it is He who teaches men to live always in their heavenly Father's sight, as He himself did;

He it is who alone fully embodies love, truth, justice, the supreme realities which mean more than earthly life:

listen; listen as He speaks!

And inasmuch as He was affronted by hatred, by betrayal, by abandonment into the hands of wicked men,

inasmuch as in His human flesh He suffered more than you can ever suffer,

since He died as you shall die, but more horribly, being given over to the dread infamy of a felon's end;

therefore did He give you an example to follow, by revealing that Death is swallowed up in Victory,

for you, being ransomed by Him, are destined and promised to Life Eternal:

therefore, my heart, listen as He speaks.

X

The Canon of our Faith

THE CREDO

All that He has come to teach me, that do I believe with all the strength of my soul! Such is the intent and purpose of the Creed.

From the earliest days of Christianity, the emission of an act of faith was a pre-requisite for being baptized. No doubt, the formulary was then very simple, something perhaps in the nature of the declaration made by the Ethiopian officer to Philip the Deacon, when he said: "I believe that Jesus Christ is the Son of God" (Acts 8:37). But it was not long before error launched itself at the principles of Christian faith, and from this there arose the necessity of stating those principles in precise and definite terms.

It was to satisfy this need that there were drawn up *Symbols,* brief affirmations, concrete propositions of belief—"the canons of our faith," as they were called in third century Africa.

The old *Apostles' Creed,* whose direct and definite statements are familiar to our private prayers, did not suit the exigencies aroused when the great heresies of the fourth century opened questions inevitably attendant upon any attempt to discern the nature of Christ in relation to the persons of the divine Trinity. So it was that, at two Councils—one held in Nicea in 325, the other at Constantinople in 381—there was drawn up

the text of a more elaborate symbol or statement of belief. It is this Creed that we find in our Sunday Masses.

First at Antioch, and then later at Constantinople, it was decided to insert the Creed in the Mass formulary. The usage spread to Spain, to France, and into the Germanies; but Rome itself did not adopt it until after the year 1000.[1]

In our own time, the use of the *Credo* is limited to Sunday Masses, to other Masses which particularly concern the whole Christian community, and to those feasts which are expressly connected with some direct evocation of one of the Symbol's clauses.[2] While the celebrant is himself saying the Creed with profound fervor, the faithful of the congregation stand to proclaim it aloud and unanimously. "Let the Creed resound," ordered a Council held at Toledo in Spain in 589, "so that the true faith may be declared in song, and that the souls of believers, in accepting that faith, may be made ready to partake, in communion, of the Body and Blood of Christ."

In the Gospel the Word has spoken to men; now Incarnate, He will come to offer Himself upon the altar. The *Credo* thus becomes a wonderful link between two parts of the Mass.

64

I WOULD that each time I join in the *Credo,*
There might re-echo the joy of my baptismal song,
Voicing aloud the strength of my faith
And my heart's cleaving to my Lord!

I would that the whys and the wherefores of my faith,
I, standing with my brethren, might proudly proclaim,
Just as once it was, and may again be
In the face of terror unleashed on the fold.

I would that my deep loyalty I might now declare
To my holy Mother, the Church, dear keeper of my faith;
For the words she has taught, she has herself learned
'Neath the unfailing shade of the radiant Spirit's wing!

XI

The Offertory

PRAYERS AT THE OFFERING

The Ante-Mass, which has now come to its conclusion, is also called "the Mass of the Catechumens," for those who were but aspirants to the faith were anciently bidden to depart from the assembly after the proclamation of the act of faith. As well as the non-baptized, sinners who were making public profession of penitence were dismissed; none but full members of the Christian band who were themselves, so to speak, "in good standing," were permitted to attend the holy mysteries which now open in the fuller sense. Within the closed company of the faithful, there were upraised a series of prayers to voice the collective intention of the Church standing on the verge of the holy of holies. Of these prayers there remain, nowadays, but three short and tantalizing reminders: the versicle *Dominus vobiscum* with its customary response, and the injunction *Oremus.*

The first sacramental act is the Offering. It is now marked by a group of six prayers. Of these one differs from day to day, being specifically adapted to the time or the festival being observed; the other five are fixed, having as their aim the presentation to God not alone of the offerings but of those who make those offerings as well. How full of meaning was the old ceremonial which marked this moment in the early church! The congregation indicated unmistakably their share in the act of offering by going themselves, in procession, to present their gifts. What were these gifts? Bread and wine, first of all; but also other edible substances, and even other things, such as gold and silver, even birds and flowers. The deacons sorted out these gifts on a special table, and they placed on one side all that would be used in the sacrifice; on the other they piled up what would be given to the poor. A responsive or antiphonal chant was sung during this procession, and it would appear that the Offertory must have been among the most striking parts of the Mass.

By the time of the Middle Ages this usage had gradually been done away with, no doubt because of the germ of possible disorder which lay within it. Our time has seen an effort at a symbolic revival of this open participation; and in some places the beautiful suggestion is made to the people that they themselves put into the ciborium the particles which are to be consecrated. There are also many other current usages which recall the primitive offertory: the collection of money has in view the same charitable end, while the community aspect is evoked whenever the custom is established of families taking turn in supplying the bread to be used. The same may be said, as well, of the offering or stipend which is given to the priest whom we request to say a special Mass for us; for in such a case the gift and the intention may be regarded as being linked. But, of course, the very essence of all these usages is comprehended in the prayerful words which the priest now says in our name.

When he holds, with both his hands, the paten on which he has placed the host, and when he lifts it up in a gesture of magnificent supplication, it is in truth our gift of all that we are and of all that we have that he now sets forth and presents to the Lord.

I WISH that this bread and this wine which the priest now offers to You, my Lord, may be in Your sight as truly bread of mine, as truly wine of mine. For just as if I were living in those earlier days when I might myself have brought them to the table set near Your altar, it is I myself who now unite in offering bread and wine to You.

It is my will to be truly a participant in Your Mass, in Your Sacrifice, in firmness of faith and in depth of feeling, in attentive devotion, and in worthy reception of this sacrament;

For I wish to join myself to this unbroken offering which, throughout the centuries, Your Church has daily held aloft before Your face.

It is my wish to be one among my fellows, to be a sharer in the society that finds its link of union in You, to be one of Your own flock, so that in seeking my own salvation I may also be of avail in effecting the salvation of all mankind.

Now, therefore, to You, my Lord, do I entrust myself, into Your hands do I give myself, so that all I pray for may come to be; so that my offering may find favor in Your sight.

XII

By Bread and Wine

THE PREPARATION OF THE BREAD AND WINE

At the Offertory there begins that setting-apart of the material substances to be offered to God, a setting-apart which will reach its culmination at the *Consecration*. It is prescribed that two kinds of material substances be thus marked for presentation to God: these are bread and wine. Such were the elements chosen by Jesus Himself at the Last Supper to be the perceptible signs of the self-immolation he there made. How fitting it is that these humble and quite ordinary fruits of the earth should be made the instrumentalities whereby the Saviour comes to mankind: bread is that staff of life of which we never outgrow the need, while in the drinking of wine our thirst is rather whetted than sated. Was it not that he might be cheered and strengthened by it that wine was given to Noah after the terrors of the Deluge?

In the beginning, the bread offered at Mass was the ordinary bread of daily use, but it was of the best kind available, marked by the Cross after having been made in the shape of rounded flat biscuits that it might the more easily be broken. From about the ninth century *azyme* bread began to be used, recalling that non-fermented, unleavened bread which Jesus, in observing the Law of Moses, would have used, and did use, at the Last Supper. The Mass wine is simply the juice of "the fruit of the vine," which in His own life-time on earth the Master was ac-

customed to drink. By a custom which dates only from the fourteenth century white wine is often used now for evident reasons of cleanliness, although these reasons are somewhat neglectful of the more striking symbol of blood which the use of red wine would afford.

In the long view of the whole matter, the bread and the wine become, from the moment they are first offered to God, symbols of Christ's body and blood; and it is as such that they are now viewed by the soul; for the Offertory anticipates, as it were, the *Consecration*. A liturgical act emphasizes this: the priest adds a little water to the wine in the chalice, so that the two liquids may blend, just as in Christ the nature of the Word and the nature of His Sacred Humanity are inseparable, just as the Master and His Church are one. During the Middle Ages it was widely believed, as well, that by this water was also figured that which came from the pierced side of the crucified Jesus; and, in a touching rite, the Greek liturgy prescribes the use of a small lancet in the Mass, whereby the host is transfixed in memory of that wounded side. "We offer unto you, O Lord, this chalice of salvation," now says the priest, signifying that in mystic manner the bread will become flesh and the wine in the chalice blood: the Sacrament is already coming into being.

IF YOU HAVE naught else to lay before the Lord, deliver unto Him at least your labors and your pain;

many are the men who have striven mightily that this fragment of bread might rest here upon the paten.

If your hands are empty and your voice stricken dumb, offer at least your wounded heart and all that it has borne;

that this chalice might hold this wine, was it not needful that the grape be crushed and yield its all?

If you have nothing but sin and bitterness, a life that is tedious and full of sharp distress,

at least hold before heaven your hands so pitiably laden, manifesting to the divine mercy your need to be received at His table.

If you lack the mere strength to pray and entreat, if there is naught in your heart but emptiness and disorder,

then silently yield into the hands of Another all your being, and you shall find in Him both Gift and Giver.

XIII

With Clean Hands

THE WASHING OF THE CELEBRANT'S HANDS

Following the Offertory at solemn Masses the priest incenses the altar, just as he had done at the beginning of the Mass of the Catechumens. This recalls the "fragrant sacrifices" beloved of Israel; and it is a ceremonial act of deep meaning. The perfume of the incense ascends to God as does a prayer. "There was another angel that came and took his stand at the altar, with a censer of gold," says the writer of the *Apocalypse,* "and incense was given him in plenty, so that he could make an offering on the golden altar before the throne, out of the prayers said by all the saints." (8:3–4).

In the event, it has now become customary at *all* Masses to carry out at this point a liturgical act which in its origin was primarily a response to a practical necessity: by the washing of his hands, which had touched the general offerings of the congregation as well as the incense-bearing thurible, the celebrant cleansed them in anticipation of taking up the bread about to become the body of Christ. It was usual, aforetime, that this washing be performed at the Epistle side of the altar where there used to stand a basin hewn from the rock of the church wall. Does not this act even now serve to maintain the old tradition of the Judaic lustral purification? It may also be regarded as having the same sense as that old-time washing in a fountain before the church door, a washing of which the people now keep the meaning by dipping their fingers in the holy water basin as they come in. But here again the symbolic sense offers its own justification, so that, as in baptism, water which cleanses the body is thought of as purifying the soul. This thought is enforced by the verse of the twenty-fifth Psalm which the priest now recites: "*Lavabo inter innocentes manus meas . . .*" I will wash my hands in innocency, my Lord, and then I will do my sacred duty at your altar.

WITHIN MY BEING there is so deep-seated a stain that not all the fountains of this world can wash it out.

That stain clings so firmly to every fibre of my being as entirely to impregnate it, having become, indeed, part of myself.

There is no one of my thoughts or actions but sharply recalls to me

that I am tainted within and without; that, despite all my distaste for evil, what I would not, that I yet do.

Is there, then, to be found any water, any water unlike the waters of this earth,

is there a stream wholly pure, chastely untainted, and everlastingly clean?

Can there be any laver so marvellously fit as to wash from my being this innermost crassness,

a laver that will cleanse the dregs of hidden shame from the darksome fen that is my soul?

All this Your grace can do, my Lord . . .

Now, therefore, let it stream upon my head, running down upon my shoulders and covering me;

may it re-effect all that was done in the baptismal font from which I rose new-born to You;

may it run down and search out all those darksome corners, hidden, unavowed, and scarce acknowledged even to myself;

may it restore to me a purity all unspotted, such a purity as marks regained childhood's clear-eyed joy.

XIV

To the Three Divine Persons

PRAYER TO THE HOLY TRINITY

When he has come back to the center of the altar the priest bows in silence. The part which he is to take in the sacrifice, properly so called, now lies immediately before him; he therefore withdraws for an instant into appropriate recollection. The prayer which he then says seems to have the form of some prayer of private devotion; and it was, as a matter of fact, unknown to the primitive Roman liturgy. Nevertheless, it is quite ancient, being commonly ascribed to St. Ambrose, the great bishop of fourth-century Milan. Its official appearance in the Mass dates from about the twelfth century; but even today the Carthusians do not make use of it in their liturgy.[1]

Suscipe, Sancta Trinitas, hanc oblationem . . . "Receive, O Holy Trinity, this oblation . . ." We may note that almost all the prayers of the Mass are addressed to the Father or to the Son, to the Father through the Son; but here direct address is made to the Trinity. This demonstrates the importance of this prayer: it offers an opportunity to take stock, as it were, of the deep meaning of the sacrifice which is about to be offered in high religious avowal of the fullness of God's divinity seated in the Blessed Trinity. Moreover, the text itself is full of suggestive significance: first it refers to several of the capital events in the life of Our Lord—His Passion, Resurrection, and Ascension. (More logically, the old rite of Lyon here begins by recalling the Incarnation and the Nativity.)[2] Then this prayer goes on to make mention of those great saints who stand before the Throne of the august Trinity as special intercessors for mankind. Thus does it recall to our minds the two determining reasons we have for the hope of glory which is in us.

80

TO BE SAVED—I do not know precisely all that this means, my Lord. What is Salvation but the fact of coming to a knowledge of all that You are? And is not this something which is beyond discerning by the fleshly eyes of mortals? Yet this much I do know—for shattering experience has so taught me—I can never be saved of myself alone.

Of You, one God in three Persons, Holy Writ tells us that no man can see Your Face and not die. In Your sight I search myself, and I find and acknowledge that I am nothing: I am but a fleeting and miserable object before the everlasting and all-powerful Fashioner of mankind; my flesh is laden with sin, my soul is tainted and stained as I kneel before the Great Exemplar, the one Model of perfection. I confess that my judgment is varying and uncertain, my comprehension but weak and vain, being indeed, no more than a feeble rush-light which vanishes in the all-consuming brilliance of that Spirit who knows and tries all that is.

Nevertheless, I know that my God took upon Himself flesh like unto my own: He lived, He suffered, and He died just as I do and shall. Yet He is not wholly like me, for did He not rise again after death, did He not rise of His own power? It is because He did so rise, and because I know it with entire certainty, that the hope of salvation swells up in my soul. It is through the Son, God in man made manifest, that I shall, one day, know the Father in the dazzling clarity of the Spirit.

And I have a cloud of witnesses—all those who have passed beyond and have gained God's presence. My hope rests upon experience and is buoyed up by it; for there once walked on earth a woman called Mary, men called John the Baptist, Peter, and Paul, and countless others. They now stand close to that Presence before whom nothing defiled may come; they stand interceding for me, inspiring me. Inasmuch as all these have known Your Grace, my Lord, why may not I?

XV

In Secret

THE SECRET PRAYERS

The third portion of the Mass is over: I have *prayed;* I have *listened;* I have *made my offering.* The priest now kisses the altar and urgently begs the congregation to unite themselves with him in order to take part in his offering, and here it is that he seems to pause in what he is doing that he may make a final and most pressing appeal to them before he proceeds to the Consecration. He does this in the words of a medieval prayer, the *Orate fratres,* which is a sort of long-drawn out *Oremus.* It expresses in marvelous fashion the full sense of this, his final injunction to the bystanders to join with heartfelt sincerity in what he is about to do: "This sacrificial act of mine is yours as well." It is as though he said: "Be mindful that I do not make this offering alone, but together with you!"

And it is as if in answer to this appeal that we have at this point in the Mass the second of the three great imprecatory invocations, the *Secrets;* the others being the *Collects* and the *Postcommunions.* Of great antiquity, harking back to the same age as the Collect, which it resembles also in style, the Secret is, like it, addressed to the Triune God in Unity, on behalf of the whole body of Christians. Why is it called *Secreta?* Is it as if, by contrast to the Collect—the prayer of the *plebs collecta*[1]—there is here signified the prayer proper to the chosen ones, to the *faithful,* as distinct from the greater assembly which had, until an earlier point in the

Mass, included the catechumens as well? Or should it rather be taken as having reference to the oblations of bread and wine which are now set apart, or secreted,[2] from the other offerings? Or does this name indicate that we here have a prayer of introduction to the *secret things,* to the King's mysteries? Whatever be the historical origin of the term, it is now generally translated as *the prayer said in secret.* For it is most quietly that the celebrant enunciates these words, as if to suggest that having now entered into the Holy of Holies, the priest, even though the representative and messenger of the people, is nevertheless, in his function, set apart from them. The straight-forward and telling phrases of the secret prayer vary according to the Mass Proper which is being used, and they express the characteristic spirit of the day being celebrated. In accordance with that ascensional, or upward-striving, note which marks the progress of the liturgical action from the beginning of the Offertory, these prayers give evidence, when they are contrasted with the Collects, of an increase in fervor and assurance. They all display one grand, dominating idea: I know that these fruits of the earth, which are my gift to God, will be returned to me after they have been touched by the fecund blessing of His inexhaustibly bounteous hand.

I know that they are my pledge or earnest of heaven, and of that everlasting life which He will give me.

84

QUIETLY DO I MURMUR this prayer as it bespeaks the feelings of my innermost heart: it is a song of hope and of comfort as I struggle with dark and oppressive fears.

My Lord, well do I know that my gift to You is less than nothing, being but a morsel of bread and a few drops of wine poured into Your Cup, while nothing could be less worthy of being accepted by You than my own miserable self.

But will you dwell upon the worth of what is offered to You? When weighed in the balance with You what is there but will be found wanting? It is only the upward thrust of joyous confidence holding out these trifling gifts to You, it is only the plea of faith that begs You to accept them, that finds favor in Your sight.

I know that in return for a single grain of wheat You can grant a most abundant harvest; for one word spoken in mercy, the fullness of Your all-embracing pardon; for a simple draught of cold water given in Your Name, that Living Water which quenches undying thirst; and that to him who takes up and bears Your Cross, You will grant Gilead's balm.

Therefore, my Lord, as, in singleness of heart and full generously, I offer You all that I have been, all that I am, and all that I shall become, I know that Your boundless Love will enrich me a thousandfold with peace, with true happiness, and with hope.

XVI

The Prologue to the Great Thanksgiving

THE PREFACE

We are approaching the climax of our worship as we begin that great prayer which now initiates the sacrificial part of the Mass, the true re-enactment of the sacrifice of the Cross. We are come to the *Canon,* that is to say as this Greek word tells us, to the part of the ceremony which is the *rule* and measure of it all, determining its lines and its whole meaning. Of great antiquity, and stemming, indeed, directly from that Last Supper which it reproduces, this *action*—to use the term which the early Christians employed—gives us pause both by reason of its architectonic magnificence and because of the stately simplicity of its formularies. The Canon can be divided into seven sections, of which the Consecration is the focal point.

Now the priest cries out to all the people: "*Sursum corda*—Lift up your hearts"; this is the moment when your thoughts should be set on God alone. The celebrant stands with uplifted hands as though he would bear aloft the compelling expectation of the congregation. With one voice the people acclaim the Lord on whom their hearts are fixed. This is just what was anciently done in the old Church of Africa in the days of that great and holy bishop, Cyprian of Carthage.

The Gospel tells us that before He blessed the wine of the Supper, Christ our Lord gave thanks to God; and this is, indeed, so essential a part of our worship that the word *Eucharist* which describes it has come to be used of the whole Sacrifice itself. Therefore is it that with *the giving of thanks* is begun the action which is the very heart of the Mass. First of all, the celebrant says—or rather he declaims—the *Preface.* How aptly does this word (which has been in use since the third century) convey the purpose of this prayer. The Preface is the introduction to the sacrifice, the eucharistic prologue, the thanksgiving which, according to the institution of Christ, must precede the Consecration.[1] It is, moreover, a reminder to us of those elaborate and abundant extemporaneous prayers which, in primitive times, faith and love brought to birth on the lips of the officiant.[2] In modern times, there has been a tendency to think of the Preface as being separate from the Canon; but it may truly be felt that to that Canon is intimately linked this prayer so pure in its style that it seems to have been born in the depths of the human heart and thence to thrust itself upward toward the Summit which is God. The Greek and Armenian churches have but one Preface to be used throughout the entire year, while at Rome there used to be a different one for each day.[3] This principle of the variable Preface is now maintained in the fifteen which our modern Missal retains, in

88

accommodation to the varying seasons and feasts of the liturgical year. All of them are constructed in similar form and style and show that they are rooted in the same motivation. They stress that the Sacrifice is offered to God, the Lord Almighty, and that this is done by, and in the Name of Jesus Christ. Each of the Prefaces, in its turn, recalls what it is that has been done by Him to effect our salvation. For the very reason that the Preface thus touches in its intention upon what is by nature ineffable, it is fitting that the angels of the heavenly court be called upon to join with us in it, and they are accordingly invoked to the greater glory of God.

CAN YOU NOW impel yourself, my heart, above your own concerns, and rise to the things of God?

Consider what hours you allot, each day, to the perishing wrecks of time, and how brief is your vigil for everlasting life.

The moment has come to be still: it is now that, in fullness of heart and with confidence unbounded,

you must draw apart and impel yourself upward!

For this much you know: these mystic rites are your own; they are the very life of your life.

This you know: there can be no greater, no truer joy for you than the joy born of this divine confrontation.

This you know: the Son of God, in taking flesh from the womb of the Virgin; Mary, in freely becoming the Mother of Sorrows; the Man-God, in deigning to live your life, to share with you the pangs of mortal death, to come, even as you shall, to the tomb;

all this they did, as you know, only for you.

All this indeed you know. Yet it is only in the long-awaited fulfillment of heavenly union that the rich floods of this knowing shall water the dry ground of your selfhood's uttermost limits.

XVII

Sanctus, Sanctus, Sanctus

THE THREE-FOLD ACCLAMATION TO THE

ALL-HOLY

How stupendous is the Glory of God! And it is with impetuous violence that this hymn, with its thrice-repeated acclamation, brusquely breaks in upon the flowing periods of the great prayer of thanksgiving. The celebrant bows low; the little bell is pealed three times; God in His holiness brings brightness to the night of our mortal days.

Not every one of the ancient liturgies knew this hymn, although its institution is attributed to St. Sixtus I who, as Pope, introduced it into the Mass in the second century. Today, it is part of all liturgies, being called the *Sanctus* among the Latins and the *Trisagion* among the Greeks.

It falls into two parts. The first of these brings to mind a mysterious passage in Isaias, wherein that prophet tells us of his vision of God (6:1–3): "I saw the Lord sitting upon a throne that towered high above me, the skirts of his robe filling the Temple. Above it rose the figures of the seraphim, each of them six-winged; with two wings they veiled God's face, with two his feet, and the other two kept them poised in flight. And

ever the same words passed between them, Holy, holy, holy is the Lord God of hosts; all the earth is full of His glory!" It is in recollection of our heritage from that old Israel of promise that we Christians still make liturgical use of the Hebrew word *Sabaoth*,[1] as we sing to the Lord of hosts.

The second part of the hymn takes up the same theme, and calls upon the Powers of Heaven to help us in glorifying the One Lord. Does not the *Hosanna in excelsis* recall the song of the angels at Bethlehem on Christmas night? And here is a reference to Christ; for this *hosanna* (another Hebrew word) is followed by the very formulary men used to salute the Messiah at His solemn entry into the holy City: "Blessed is He who comes in the name of the Lord" (Mark 11: 9–10).

Now is God in man made manifest truly come among us. As the words of this hymn are said, He enters into the core of this sacramental action just as, aforetime, He came into Jerusalem, there to ascend His throne, the throne of the Cross.

WHEN I PONDER within my heart, my Lord, on Your Glory and on the limitless power that lies within Your hand;

when I consider the vastness of Your creation, and peer into endless vistas of space; when I recollect that behind all that is, behind all that has been, You are;

when I reflect that for uncounted aeons of years, Your Spirit has hovered unsearchably over the destiny of men;

then do I ask, how—even were all the angelic choirs to lend me their voices that I might more worthily hymn Your unexampled holiness—

then do I ask, as I bend in love while my mind reels before the unfathomed mystery of Your nature,

then do I ask how it can be that You, centering in Yourself the Perfection of all Glory, nevertheless regard my nothingness;

how it is that You are mindful of me and reveal to me the secret of Yourself and all Your being as You suffer a drop of Your divine blood to fall on the face of a sinner?

XVIII

The Church at the Foot of the Cross

THE REMEMBRANCE OF THE LIVING

Te igitur . . .—"Wherefore, O most merciful Father, we humbly beseech You, through Your Son, Jesus Christ, our Lord, that you would be pleased to receive these gifts, these presented offerings . . ." It is in these words that the brilliant interruption made by the *Sanctus* in the unfolding of the ideas first expressed in the *Preface* is bridged over (as the word *igitur*[1] indicates), in order that there may be resumed the series of prayers leading directly to the *Consecration*. Here, indeed, begins the Canon strictly so-called, and it was this consideration which moved the miniaturists of the Middle Ages to paint the initial letter T of *Te igitur* in such wondrous style. How well does this letter figure the Cross; and it is, in fact, the origin of those Crucifixion scenes which are found in most Missals at this point in the text. The hour of the Sacrifice has come; the celebrant now moves more solemnly than hitherto, all his motions are charged with a consciousness of their mystic meaning as he progresses from action to action, now joining his hands, now raising his eyes to heaven, again kissing the altar once more; and then, having made the three-fold sign of the Cross over the *oblata*, he finally extends his hands, palms downward, over the chalice and the host, in the manner of one who gives testimony under oath.

There are five prayers said in a low voice before the Consecration of the Elements. Their sequence is not wholly smooth, nor is it devoid of awkwardness and interruption; for they are the result of a series of dislocations and developments covering several centuries. For example, the first of them (*Te igitur*) and the last (*Quam oblationem*) belong, most certainly, to the Canon in its very oldest form; the list of saints who are called to memory (in the *Communicantes*) dates from the third century; while other parts and phrases can be fixed at about the sixth century, with the exception of the *Hanc igitur*, which is even later. Nevertheless, it is one grand and over-ruling idea which has determined the whole train of thought we find here: it is that of the fellowship or communion of all Christians in God.

As Christ now makes ready to mount the Cross, the priest states the full purpose of the Sacrifice which is offered for the salvation of the Church militant on earth, and to the glory of the Church triumphant in heaven. He now calls forth and ranges round about the altar the whole company of baptized Christians, their leaders and exemplars at their head; he calls forth all who suffered and strove here below to lengthen the blessed shadow which the Cross casts over the sins of the world; and he calls, as well, on those

who are now sharers in that glory to which we look. In first place stands the glorious Virgin, Mary the Mother of God, the Consoler of Men. As a matter of fact, the whole Christian community (the word *familia* is actually used) is conceived of as being now assembled here where the sacrificial prayer is making into a present reality the rapidly approaching moment when, by transubstantiation, the whole substance of the offerings will become the whole substance of the Body and Blood of Christ Our Lord.

Lord, all we stand here in Your sight, we Your witnesses throughout the world, united in the brotherhood of faith and of hope,

all we, Lord, who in Your holy will and grace are sons of the Church You so deeply love.

Here is Your Vicar who most fully bears in Your name, the burden and the care of all the churches;

here is Your flock; men good and bad, the strong of heart and those who are fearful; all are come together to await Your blessing.

And by their side stand those who even now do look upon Your face: here are Your apostles, Your martyrs, Your beloved, Your chosen ones.

In sacramental union, they are one with us; despite our failings and our sinfulness, they join to our offering the fellowship of the saints.

All we are here, agonizing Jesus, seeing You torn with the bitterness of unmerited pain and woe,

we are here in the certain hope that by Your word the bread and the wine we offer are made the earnest of our redemption.

Now, Lord, we pray that, just as in that final moment of Your earthly life You gazed in love on Mary and on John,

You will now turn Your face to Your whole church, standing with heart overflowing in love and supplication, beside the Cross whereon Your Sacrifice is wrought.

XIX

This is My Body

THE ELEVATION OF THE HOST

Vain is every attempt to explain, on merely historical grounds, the signification of this high liturgical act which is the very culmination of the Mass. The Church says nothing of herself; but, hiding herself behind the Person of the Christ, uses no words, employs no gestures, but His own. The *Consecration* and the Supper are one. The Consecration reproduces and extends the mystic memorial of the Last Supper when Jesus, who was facing betrayal and death, freely offered his Body and His Blood for the redemption of mankind. In this lies the essence of the Mass as it has existed from the days of the early Christians; for the book of the Acts and the apostolic Letters offer more than one testimonial to its celebration. In the beginning, to this rite was joined that of the fraternal supper, the *Agapé* or love-feast of the community;[1] but out of respect for the holier rite, the connection between it and the Agapé was broken at about the end of the first century.

Christ, therefore, is seen to be the author of the form, the actions, the very words of the Consecration. In this moment, the priest quite literally becomes Christ Himself: his own personality is blotted out; it is absorbed in that of the everlasting Priest who is, at one time, the offered victim and the supreme officiant. For this reason it is Our Lord's own movements, as reported by the Gospel, which determine what the priest does: just as the Master did, the celebrant now raises his eyes on high; as Jesus blest the bread, so does he. (The genuflexion which the priest inserts here is no more than a personal mani-

festation of his adoration of God now sacramentally present.) The words, too, which the celebrant says are words used by Jesus, "those great and wondrous words," as St. Athanasius called them, those words which, in their simple directness, offer a contrast to the rich formularies wherein they are enshrined. It is as though God would show that He has no need for a multiplicity of verbiage.

Nevertheless, what we have in the liturgical formularies is no merely textual reproduction of the evangelical account: something has been added in the course of the centuries.[2] Such are certain adjectives, as those which describe the hands of Our Lord as *sanctas ac venerabiles* (holy and worthy of respect), or the word (inspired by Psalm 22:5) by which the chalice is called *praeclarum,* or glorious. None of these additions is of much importance. Since the medieval period we find, in the midst of the consecratory formula for the wine, the words: *Mysterium fidei,* the mystery or sacrament of faith.[3] Their meaning is that here shines forth the essence of the Christian faith; for now *truly, really, substantially* (such as the Tridentine terminology), the bread and the wine are become the Body and the Blood of Jesus Christ.

It is because of the greatness of this mystery[4] that it has been so panoplied with solemnity. Especially has this been so since the twelfth century when heresy cast doubt upon the real presence. The thrice-rung bell, the clouds of incense, the lighting of a third

candle,[5]—all are tributes to the Holy Presence. Particularly does the Elevation affirm this Presence in a magnificent gesture which, at once, raises to heaven and shows to the whole congregation, the bread which has become the Body of Christ. Before bowing down in profound adoration, the devout soul looks up in fullness of faith and hope at the little host which veils the greatest of all mysteries.

HERE BEFORE YOUR FACE, devoutly I adore You:
My mind divests itself of all but You;
This bread on which I gaze, this bread raised now on high,
It is You, Yourself, Your very flesh: this I believe and trust.

As now, in silence, naught but You I see,
Grant me to cleave more firmly to my faith;
Subdue my will, my heart, my reason; and, by Your grace,
May all the love you've showered on me, flow back to You.

XX

This is My Blood

THE ELEVATION OF THE CHALICE

It is not enough to adore God-made-man who is now present in the host. Nor are we to be satisfied by an entire acceptance of the mystery of transubstantiation. What must be done is to turn in full realization toward the action which now is being wrought at the altar. This is a purely sacrificial act; and it must generally be admitted that the wine evokes, in a more striking manner than does the bread, the force of the sacrificial act by recalling the blood so freely shed on Calvary's hill by the victor Victim. At this point, we are become witnesses of Christ's act of immolation. We are, as a matter of fact, more intimately united to it than are mere witnesses; for it is we ourselves who offer to the Father this Lamb who now mystically sacrifices Himself: we are partakers, sharers, participants, in His act.

This puts us in touch with what has been, from time out of memory, recognized as being the core and the center of the oldest religious tradition. It is by the shedding of blood in reparation that man has ever appeased supernatural Power. In the days of old Israel every fault of whatsoever kind, be it one attaching moral or even merely ceremonial defilement, had to be blotted out in blood. *Sine sanguine non fit remissio:* without the shedding of blood, there is no forgiveness of sin.[1]

Yet it is evident that the mere sacrificial act of itself, unqualified by purpose, by supplicatory prayer, by participation, is of itself unavailing. "Is not this cup we bless" asks St. Paul, "a participation in Christ's blood?" (I Cor., 10:16). The words themselves by which the wine is consecrated are much more explicit than are those of the consecration of the bread, and they have the effect of indicating very forcibly that we are here concerned with a means of attachment between God and man, with a "New Covenant." Here again we confront the *mysterium fidei,* the mystery or sacrament of faith; it is by sharing in the Victim's offering that man can find pardon for his own sins.

Just as he did with the host, the priest lifts the chalice and shows it to the people, after he has blessed it. This is a more recent usage than the elevation of the host; for during the Middle Ages chalices were generally wider than those we use today, and hence more difficult to hold aloft in due reverence; but it is clear that the purpose of this elevation is a similar one: it is a tribute to the *Presence* of the Blood of Christ.

At this time we should join to the Life which is offered sacrificially on Calvary, our own life, by uniting in full oblation; for our own life is without meaning unless it be thus given to its Giver.

TRULY DO I BELIEVE that this Blood now offered in the Chalice
Is Your own, once given to the Father;
It is truly the same as that which spurted under the scourge,
Most truly the Blood that flows forever from Your wounds.

Grant, Crucified Jesus, that in its flowing
Your Blood may mingle with my own, unworthy though I am;
Grant that I, too, may give my life to God, and join
My sacrifice to Yours, my life thus being oned with Your own.

XXI

In Remembrance...

THE SUPPLICES

After the consecration of the bread and wine, Jesus said: *Haec quotiescumque feceritis, in mei memoriam facietis,* "As often as you do this, do it in remembrance of me." Therefore, doubtless already in the time of the Apostles, and in any case before the close of the second century, the Church had here inserted in the Liturgy a Memorial or Anamnesis (*Unde et memores . . .*), to which there were added, but shortly thereafter, two supplicatory prayers (*Supra quae propitio . . .* and *Supplices te rogamus . . .*). In the ensemble of these three prayers there is evident a grave sobriety in which are recognized the accents of primitive Christianity.

To what does this Memorial or Anamnesis have reference? Certainly to the Passion,[1] for that it is which the Oblation of the Supper evokes. And it is for this reason that the celebrant now signs Host and Chalice with the Cross, and that according to some particular liturgical uses,[2] he here extends his arms in cross-like fashion. ". . . it is the Lord's death that you are heralding," St. Paul has told us, "whenever you eat this bread and drink this cup . . ." (I Cor., 11:26). This is then certainly a recalling of His death; but it recalls, as well, Christ's Resurrection and His glorious Ascension. Therefore in the anamnesis we have a sort of resumé or summing-up of the whole Mass: it underlines the whole meaning of the Mass that it may the more fully reveal it.

The Oblata upon which we begged God's blessing are now become one with "that pure, holy, unspotted Oblation, the sacred bread of life everlasting, the cup of redemption." We turn to God and are bold to say that these gifts can now be received by Him; for they are no longer unworthy of Him. And did He not, aforetime, receive the sacrifices of Abel, of Abraham, and of Melchisedech, all of which were no more than types or figures of His Son's sacrifice? Thus does the past indicate what is to be.

Now bowing low in supplication, the priest begs of the Almighty Lord that He would give to us, in the Eucharistic Communion which we are later to share, that Christ whom we have here set forth in His sight. This is the intent of the prayer which begins with the word *Supplices.* Of this most meaningful and mysterious prayer Innocent III remarked that human understanding can scarce apprehend its full significance. Before the face of God's ineffable Majesty, the only acceptable Offering is laid upon the heavenly Altar, and the angelic liturgy completes what human worship had begun: thus is the Sacrifice made on earth consummated in heaven.

And we may feel assured that, if we have but taken thought to entrust them to Him, it is our hopes and our fears, the best part of our very selves, which the Sacred Victim now carries into the Father's Heart.

HOW GREAT had been my joy
Had I been one among the throngs
That gathered round the Lake while Jesus spoke!

What chill had struck my soul had I been there,
When from the tomb, responding to His simple call,
The answering Lazarus came forth!

Would not His words have burned within my breast
Had I been there, when at the Table, long ago,
He first gave thanks and broke the Holy Bread?

Would not my heart have cracked in tears and pain
Had I stood near His Cross, on Calvary's hill,
With Magdalene, Our Lady, and St. John?

And, had I seen, that Easter morn,
The rollèd stone, the empty tomb,
Would not my soul have overflowed in hope new born?

But hearken now, my soul: in all these words and acts,
Even in prayers that your distraction failed to hear,
In all are now, by mystic drama here enacted,
The saving floods, unfathomed yet, of your Redemption!

Your kneeling at this Altar is no empty form;
Love grips you here: your life's the price of yielding.
Your dry roots now unveil; and let them watered be
While Jesus wraps you in the mantle of His blood.

XXII

Our Dead and We Sinners

THE COMMEMORATION OF THE DEAD

Is it for ourselves that we are offering this Sacrifice? It can never be too often repeated that the Mass is rooted in fellowship, in a union with Christ the Son of God, and with men, our brethren. At the very beginning of Mass, by the Collect, and later, by the formularies preparatory to the Consecration, we were reminded of this; and now again two further intercessory prayers re-enforce the will which should be in us for brotherly union.

Before Christ was raised aloft in the Elevation, the Church militant and the Church triumphant were assembled around the Cross; but the Liturgy now pauses to consider the sorrowing Church as prayer is offered for the dead and for sinners.

Prayer for the dead is of great antiquity. It was known to the Synagogue; and St. John Chrysostom assures us that the tradition has passed to us directly from the Apostles. Nevertheless, the actual *Commemoration* of the dead, as we now have it, is like the other Commemorations something of late introduction into the Mass. It is not found in manuscripts of as late as the eleventh century. We may ask then why it was placed here at a point of such importance in the ceremony? The Fathers of the Church had already given the reason; and it is St. Cyril of Jerusalem who tells us that we ought pray for those in greatest need just when our prayer is most efficacious. Such indeed are those who, although they have passed death's Portal, still await the final revelation of refreshment, light, and peace.

The mere mention of the Souls in Purgatory should provoke us to thought of ourselves, for our own death is but a thing delayed; and it is we who are the future tenants in that state of purgation. It is for this reason that the celebrant passes quickly from the dead to us; and he fervently begs the divine loving kindness for us who are sinners (*nobis quoque peccatoribus*), in words so simple and direct as to indicate the antiquity of the tradition upon which they rest.

And, as he had done before the Consecration at the Commemoration of the Living, the celebrant calls again for the aid of intercessors, and he names here another group of saints and martyrs.[1] They are witnesses and pledges of the glory that shall be ours. Thus for the third time, and in a most definitive manner, do we find evoked that grand and wondrous reality of Christian faith, the doctrine of the Communion of Saints, which is our fellowship with the blessed.

112

NOW THAT MY PRAYER is no longer my prayer alone, but has been voiced by the divine lips of Your Crucified Son,

allow me, my Lord, in trusting confidence to put before You the plight of my brethren in You, my brethren who yet walk in the night of this mortal life:

for all whom I love; for those whom I have scarce loved at all but now join together in my heart's remembrance;

for the long generations of Christians whose prayers have been, in earlier days, borne up to You, even as now mine are;

for those who are dead, as I myself shall one day be; for those whose present faults bespeak their need of atonement's sharpest anguish;

for all with whom I soon shall be united; for all whose only hope is fixed upon Your holy Cross;

for all I beg Your saving Grace, for them and for myself. And grant, my Lord, that the offering of Your blood may pledge assuagement of that death and trial which are the wages of my sin.

XXIII

Thanksgiving

THE LITTLE ELEVATION

The Canon of the Mass here comes to its term. The few phrases which now bring to a close the long series of prayers introduced by the Preface are simple in their appearance; but, as is generally true in the liturgy, they are all the more weighty in their significance. In the first of these, which opens with the words *Per quem . . .*, we say to the Lord: "It is in Christ that You have given enduring life to all these good things; in Him that You have made them holy and useful; in Him that You bless them and give them to us." Are we to look upon this formulary as a mere resumé of the Canon, designed to bring it to a formal end? Or is it rather the remnant of some antique blessing, directed not alone to the bread and the wine, but as well to milk and honey, to the fruit of the vine, or to the newborn lambs, or to the yield of the new bean crop? It is at just this point in the rite that on Holy Thursday there is still hallowed the oil with which the sick are anointed.[1] In any case, there is no mystery about the *meaning* of this formulary. The result of the mediation of the Incarnate God, who offers Himself for the salvation of the whole world, is that the divine creative power is ever renewing holiness, grace, and love in all God has made.

By a special liturgical act the priest now appropriately expresses God's having made holy, having raised above their natural state, the things of created existence. This act is called the *Little* (or *Minor*) *Elevation,* and attention is drawn to it by the ringing of the acolyte's bell.[2] The celebrant raises host and chalice slightly at the same time. In the early Church this was the only Elevation in the Mass; for, as we know, the Elevation at the Consecration dates only from the Middle Ages. This Elevation is even more full of meaning than is the Great (or Major) Elevation; but its intent is different. It is not now to the people that the Oblata are presented: they are here held aloft to God, for the bread and the wine are become the Body and the Blood of His divine Son.

In the full sense of the term, and more expressly than are any of the prayers which precede the Consecration, this liturgical act is a *Thanksgiving*. The words which the priest says make this clear: *Per ipsum . . .* "Through Whom (i.e., Christ), by Whom, and with Whom, in the unity of the Holy Ghost, all honor and glory be unto You, O Father Almighty, world without end." It is through Christ our Mediator, in union with Him, and in a sense absorbed or incorporated in Him, that we His ransomed ones will partake with all His creation in the blessed praise of the Holy Trinity for ever. The *Amen* which closes this sublime prayer is without doubt the most significant Amen in the entire course of the Mass. This was anciently the only time that Amen was said during the old Canon; and here the word is used in its most complete and extensive sense. Let us therefore say it together, with heart-felt fervor: "So be it."

116

NOW IS ALL CREATION ransomèd, and there rests upon us the joy of unimaginable promise!

This is a promise of everlasting renewal: the seven ages of creation are refreshingly re-enacted!

All now is purified, truth reigns again, and the world around me is become once more as it was in the beginning; the heart broken by sorrow is healed in love.

A wheaten host, a cup of wine, raised to the Incarnate God in sacrificial offering, bespeak the re-awakening of all terrestrial things to their destined glory; and the marvelous glad light of the Trinity puts the darksome night to flight.

In a sacramental gesture which is beyond my power to understand, I raise up and offer to You, my Lord, all that is good; for all this is Your creation and belongs not to me, but to You alone;

and I know that by this sacrament there is brought to pass my salvation, destined from the beginning of time and perduring for ever.

Grant that I may be open to all the instrumentalities of Your Grace which this fleeting world offers in the days of my sojourning here;

make holy, with Your blessing, all that I am and might wish to be, all that I have, and all that I would surrender in the Love of Christ.

Grant, too, that I may respond in my heart with fitting joyousness to all Your boundless Love which dowers its gifts upon me!

XXIV

The Pater Noster

THE LORD'S PRAYER

The last act of the liturgical drama now begins; this fifth act is the conclusion of all. I have *prayed;* I have *listened to the Word;* I have made my *offering;* I have *joined in the Sacrifice;* now it is my turn to *receive.* At the sacrificial table I shall be united in Communion with Jesus.

The course of the liturgy enters upon this its last phase in a somewhat unexpected manner. There is first said a very touching and most ancient formulary (one alluded to already in the fourth century by St. Jerome), which asserts that were it not for the express command of Our Lord we should by no means presume to utter what we are about to say. This introduction is recited by the celebrating priest with his hands joined in a way which symbolizes a strong sense of unity—unity with God in Christ, unity, as well, with our brethren. Then he extends his hands, and having fixed his eyes upon the sacred Host, he solemnly says the *Our Father.* This is the Lord's own prayer, the prayer that encompasses all others. St. Luke has given us an account (11:2–4) of how Jesus, but a short time before He suffered, taught this prayer to His disciples in re-

sponse to their request: "Lord, teach us how to pray." Was this from a balcony in Ephrem or on the slopes of Mt. Olivet? Was it a prayer He had already used after the Sermon on the Mount, as St. Matthew's text suggests (6:9–13)? There cannot be any doubt that it expresses the heart of Our Lord's Gospel: this prayer is His spiritual legacy to us. The custom of reciting the *Pater* at the Eucharist is of great antiquity, and it may be of even apostolic origin: many are the allusions made to this custom in the writings of the old Church Fathers, and St. Augustine regarded it as something long-established in his own time. In the sixth century St. Gregory the Great, while pope, decreed that this prayer should be said just prior to the Communion, and he was surely guided by high inspiration and profound insight in this decision. What, after all, is the Holy Communion but the very sacrament of unity? And in preparation for it what is more desired than the charity or love of God and of our fellow men which the *Pater* arouses in us?

Before we partake of the Body of Christ it is fitting that we share in His spirit.

120

I WOULD, my Lord, say no longer distractedly or in merely routine fashion the prayer which You have taught me. This is the prayer said, down the centuries, by countless numbers of Your followers. They have never grown tired of obeying Your injunction to repeat it. I would now say it slowly and with as much awareness and consideration as though I were listening when You first taught men its words.

You tell me that God is my Father, not only my Master and my King; that He shows Himself to me not as the Mighty God upon whose face no man may gaze, not as the God of hosts, terrifying in the majesty of His justice; but rather as the Father who has raised me to sonship with You; making me an heir to His kingdom; that, despite His power and His glory I may confidently rely on His love of me.

Father, I pray You to keep us ever in Your sight; be as near to us on earth as You are to those who have entered into Your heavenly kingdom. Be with me by the bright light of Your glory in my soul; rule my spirit; and make my heart overflow with love. Be with me in Your power, establishing the kingdom of Your justice. Be with me in the open showing to me of Your will, so that I may strive joyously to accomplish it.

I ask You to sustain me in this life for as long as You will, and to grant me to earn my bread. Each day may I act with complete trust in Your providential care of me, and may I thus eat the bread of brotherhood, sharing with my fellows not only the bread which nourishes the body, but that upon which the soul is fed as well; for it is that Living Bread come down from heaven which alone can satisfy our hunger.

I ask You, once more, to forgive me all that I have done amiss; for the weight of my transgressions is more than I can bear. In the face of Your loving kindness to me, may I ever remember to conform my own conduct to it; may I be generous, ready to forgive others with brotherly love, just as You are to all of us.

Grant that temptation in the battles of my daily life may never be too much for my puny strength, as I go from one mortal trial to another; spare me those heavy trials which break the spirit, those troubles which distress the heart; and do not deliver me over to the enemy who dwells in my own evil inclinations. Father, now as the Blood of Your Son is about to bring me Your grace, Father, I beg You to have mercy upon me!

XXV

The Broken Bread

THE BREAKING OF THE HOST

After He had broken bread, the bread which He had blessed and made holy, Jesus said to His disciples: "Take and eat." The Holy Communion is thus indicated to be an integral part of the Mass, and the logical and indispensable completion of the Consecration. (It is, therefore, a mistake to sunder them by seeking, without real necessity, to communicate apart from Mass, or to withdraw from the progress of the liturgical action of the Mass into selfishly personal meditation as though one could thus better attain the union with Christ which Mass affords!)

Long ago in Israel, under the Old Law, "the Feast of the Most High" was a part of sacrificial worship, and the participants ate of the victim after some parts of it had been burned upon the altar, and the fumes had been wafted on high: thus to have joined in the divine feast by accepting the sacred aliments was an act pleasing to Almighty God. To an even greater extent, under the New Law, the Sacred Banquet possesses a power to unite its participants to God. Has not Christ Himself said, "My flesh is real food, my blood is real drink"? (John 6:56). At the Last Supper, the Apostles assuredly ate the bread and drank the wine the Master had blessed; in Apostolic times, the baptized Christians gathered together in the *Agapé,* which was at once a supper of fraternal love and of liturgical communion. Even later on, when the Supper and the Communion were no longer joined together, it was customary to keep up the lively remembrance of the banquet.[1] In our own time we have perhaps lost this feeling of sharing in a Common Supper, despite the fact that such a realization expresses so strikingly the concept of that brotherly union in God which is so necessary to the fruitful reception of the Holy Sacrament. Yet even now, the actions and the words of the priest awake in our hearts inspiring echoes of past usage.

First the celebrant, in the words of a very old prayer, takes up again and develops further the idea on which the *Pater* had closed: he recalls in the *Libera nos* that it is by Christ that we are delivered. The priest then raises the Host and breaks it into two parts, and after placing one of the two halves on the paten, he breaks off a small portion of the other and puts it into the chalice. These three acts of the *Fraction* are full of significance. The divided host represents the bread broken at the Last Supper (the Jews always broke, and never *cut,* their bread): it was in the act of breaking bread that the Risen Lord was made known to the disciples at Emmaus. According to the mystical interpretation devised in the Middle Ages, this represents the Body of Christ being broken during His Passion; but, above all, by this act is figured the distribution of His sacramental Body to His brethren. The particle set on one side recalls the old rite of the *Sancta;* a particle consecrated at a previous Mass used always be reserved until this time by way of enforcing the idea that the Mass is one; it is a perpetuation of the Mass said before, and it is continued by the Mass which will follow.[2] And, finally, the little

124

piece which is dropped into the Chalice, according to a rite which goes back to the fourth century, is a symbol of the Body and Blood of the Risen Lord united as a pledge of our own resurrection to everlasting life. Others explain it as an affirmation of the perfect union in Christ of divine and human nature. However, it has also been regarded at all times as a representation of the manner in which everyone of us is conjoined to our brethren within the bosom of the Church: we are each part of the other, just as this little particle of Bread dissolves in the Wine.

MY LORD, this is the very bread that was broken by You at the Last Supper, and was there given by Your own hands to Your apostles; this is the bread that Your martyrs shared, one with another, before they were themselves crushed and broken by the teeth of wild beasts as the wheat is crushed under the grindstone;

this is the bread partaken of by the long line of Your saints which stretches from age to age in an unending union of love and fellowship;

this is the same bread which, even now, is being renewed everywhere upon the earth in a great Mass that never ends.

Grant, therefore, that I may so receive this living bread as to recall that I am not alone, but am joined in real fellowship with all Your followers;

grant, O Lord Christ, that just as You give Yourself in every least morsel of this bread, grant that I may share Your own love for those who know You and for those who know You not;

grant that I may be thus ever more firmly linked to redeemed humanity, to all who are ransomed by Your Blood, that so I may fulfill the purpose for which You made Your Sacrifice.

XXVI

In the Blood of the Lamb

THE AGNUS DEI

"Sheep led away to the slaughter-house, lamb that stands dumb while it is shorn; no word from him." It was thus that the prophet Isaias, in a well-known passage (53:7), proclaimed the Messiah; and the Baptist took up this strain when he cried out, at the coming of Jesus: "Look, this is the Lamb of God; look, this is he who takes away the sin of the world" (John 1:29).

Again does the liturgy recur to the symbolism of the lamb in placing upon our lips a three-fold plea in the words of the *Agnus Dei*. These invocations are in the tradition set for the children of old Israel by Moses when he required that they mark the post of their doors with the blood of a lamb on that far-off paschal night while they were yet in Egypt. It was in this sign that they were spared by the Lord's Angel.

From the viewpoint of liturgiological history, it seems that the *Agnus Dei* is either the remnant of, or a substitute for, some old litany formerly sung while the consecrated Bread was being broken in preparation for its distribution among the attendants at Mass. This was sometimes a very protracted ceremony. The invocation here of the Lamb of God arose at first in the Eastern Church, and it was a Syrian pope, St. Sergius I, who authoritatively established the custom at Rome, toward the close of the seventh century. The meaning of the three straight-forward pleas to the Lamb of God is evident. Was not Israel protected by the paschal lamb; and is not the Lamb that is sacrificed the pledge of the reconciliation, thus cemented, of man with God?

It is, however, in the final words of this three-fold invocation that we may precisely discern how the love of God is found; for whereas to the first and second cries of *Agnus Dei* the response is "have mercy upon us," the plea that follows the final invocation is "grant us peace." It is on the heels of these words that the celebrant now prays that the Church may be brought to peace and unity; and here it is that, in solemn Masses, there takes place the lovely rite of the *Pax*. The giving of the kiss of peace is rooted in the practice of Our Lord and His apostles; it was thought by the primitive Christians to be something of prime importance; and it is a fault in Christians of our own time that they fail to observe it.

Once more do the words and acts prescribed by the liturgy underline that special lesson which the Mass tirelessly teaches: if we sincerely desire that God keep us in that peace which is an assurance of His love, then must we love one another!

MY LORD, there is but one sign by which You shall know me when You come in judgment, seated on the clouds of heaven and surrounded by the blinding light of Your glory in which all hidden things will lie revealed.

That sign will then be of even greater avail against the angels of divine wrath than were the marked door-posts of Israel;

it is the sign of which we read in the Apocalypse that Your servants bear it on their faces as it were a seal of their devotion to You;

it is the sign of Your loving kindness, known indeed to me, even though my heart does not wholly own it:

it is the mark and sign of the Lamb, the mark by which Your Blood will blot out forever all the hatred and spiritual unrest seated in my heart;

it is the sign of peace, of shared pardon, of brotherly affection; the sign of Your own love for us shared in by every one of us.

Ah, grant me, my Lord, a longing for this sign, that I may be marked with it, ineffaceably, in the innermost depth of my soul;

and grant that in the strength of Your sign, the mark of the Lamb, I may gain for You the whole world, that world which You have promised to those who are gentle and forbearing.

XXVII

The Celebrant's Communion

THE PRIEST RECEIVES THE HOLY COMMUNION

It is now that the celebrant makes ready to partake of the Communion, by saying two prayers which are full of fervor. In one he begs that Christ, the giver of life, will grant salvation to His servant and join him to Himself; in the other he professes his own deep unworthiness in the face of this un-thought of gift, and he begs that it may not work to his condemnation.[1] Although these prayers are most beautiful, they are rather subjective in tone and they do not belong to the main line of thought in the Mass which is, as we know, the enforcement of that primary intention that the whole Christian family be drawn together and associated one with another in the liturgical action. They are prayers of private piety, as their relatively recent introduction into the Ordinary demonstrates; they date from only about the tenth century.[2] Nevertheless, they afford each one of us an opportunity to test within his own individual selfhood that will for a general union, a shared participation, which underlies the whole Mass.

The Communion of the celebrating priest is an indispensable and essential part of every Mass. So necessary is it that if, through some unforeseen occurrence, the celebrant should be unable to communicate, another priest must take his place as soon as possible, and must consume the Sacred Elements in his stead. What sort of sacrifice would that be which was left incomplete? It is with the celebrant and, as it were, beside him, that each one of us ought fulfill the Sacrifice! The priest takes our place; he sacrifices for us. Do not the words which he pronounces express the very sentiments which rise up from the deep places of our own hearts?

In confession of our unworthiness we recall what was said by the centurion at Capharnaum; in words of gratitude we declare our wonder before these fruitful gifts of God; in words of confidence we mark the fulfillment of our worship: all unworthy as I am, I partake of everlasting life in sharing the Body and the Blood of Christ, the ever-living God . . .

I AM ABASED in Your sight as my soul hungers and thirsts for You;

my whole being awaits You in the silent stillness in which You come to me.

Never before have I so realized my unworthiness, my wretched unfitness—it is truly boundless;

never before has the intolerable sense of this unworthiness pressed so heavily upon me;

never before have I seen so clearly the truth that of myself I am nothing, that of myself I am powerless:

it is therefore in an entire recognition of my own insignificance that I kneel before You in my deep distress and tear from myself the veils of vain pretense;

for it is to You alone that I do wholly trust myself: I know that You will not cast me off.

I believe that by Your coming to me You will grant me strength and fullness of life.

I believe that, in Your Word, whatever is broken within me will be healed, whatever is unclean will be made again pure.

I believe that in this Host and in that Cup You are truly present—my God, it is with every energy of my soul that I trust and believe in You!

XXVIII

The Communion of the People

THE CONGREGATION APPROACH THE

HOLY TABLE

It is now that, in their turn, the assistants at Mass come to receive their God, to be united to Him; for to communicate is more than merely to receive. At first the distribution of the Sacred Elements was done at the same table where the *Agapé*[1] had been held, and the clergy gave them to those who were about the table; but after the fourth century it was the congregation which went solemnly toward the altar, that "Holy Table" whose very name recalls the Table of the Last Supper. In primitive times, the consecrated Bread was put into the palm of the communicant's hand, and in the mind of the early Fathers this signified the sanctification of the human senses. Then the faithful would drink, in turn, from a common cup. Communion under the two kinds—by reception of both bread and wine—is even yet the rule among the Greeks; and it persisted widely in the West until about the twelfth century, not being, in fact, officially suppressed until the action of the Council of Constance in 1418.

In earlier times, when those who were present at Mass showed a more manifest sense of participation in the service, it was not customary that the course of the liturgical action be interrupted here by each one saying the *Confiteor* to himself; rather was it at this moment that, in solemn Masses, the singing of the *Communion Anthem* was the unified act of the whole assemblage.

Kneeling and in turn, we now receive into our mouths the Bread of Life. As he administers the host to each communicant, the celebrant says, "May the Body of Our Lord Jesus Christ bring your soul to everlasting life. Amen."

In more simple terms, the ancient church —that of St. Augustine's day—used the briefer formulary, *Corpus Christi,* "This is the Body of Christ;" and it is, indeed, by these words that I know my time of waiting to be over, for my hope is now made into a reality which fulfills the deepest needs of my faith and my love.

THERE IS NEITHER SPEECH nor language—not even the language by which heart speaks to heart—fit to express all that I would now say; my joy is beyond speech.

I feel the light of Your Face shining upon me, my innermost being responds to the warmth of Your love;

You are mine, and I am Yours, wholly made one in this Sacrament: my soul worships You in stillness.

No merely human sense of gratitude even begins to take account of this gift so far above the feebleness of human insight;

no love can ever equal the Love which caused You to make Your sacrifice;

every proffered gift, every good intent, when looked at in the light of Your example and of Your offering of Yourself, is seen to be as naught.

Therefore, my Lord, what is there that I can offer You? What can I find to say to You? It is only Yourself that is worthy of You; Yourself whom I have now received in the silence of my soul.

I would now ask You, as I look back to that day of my childhood when I innocently bade You welcome in the very first of my Communions,

I would now ask You that You make me to be what it is You wish me to be, that You keep me as You would have me be;

I ask that I may share in Your own Sacrifice, and that You will be with me as I carry my Cross, as I go from sorrow to joy, from hope to fear;

I ask You to live within my soul, to possess me wholly and to remain the moving force in all that I shall do throughout my life. My God, bear me as a child in Your arms.

XXIX

In the Hand of God

THE BLESSING

The Communion over, the Mass seems to come to a close all at once; and there are some who have felt disturbed by this: they would have wished for more time in which to prolong their personal acts of devotion. It is true that the thankful prayers of a soul just visited by Christ are among the very best prayers that can be offered to God. The Church indeed counsels us to make such prayers at this time. Nevertheless, it seemed to the early Christians that the whole Mass was a continued *thanksgiving,* and that after having been made holy by the presence of the sacramental body within himself, the individual Christian could best prolong that thanksgiving by his practice of the love of his fellow men, by the acceptance of the joys and the sorrows of his own lot, by maintaining his devotional fervor.

There are two levels of meaning indicated by the prayers which are said after the Communion. In the first prayers we ask that God will grant that His gifts may do their destined work in us by keeping us in purity of life; by assuring, as one prayer movingly puts it, that what we have received in the time of mortality, may endure in our souls as an everlasting renewal of life. On the whole, this sums up the meaning of the *Ablution Prayers* which, for about thirteen hundred years, have been said while the priest cleanses the traces of the holy Body and Blood which may chance to remain on his own lips or fingers, or in the chalice. Such, also, is the signification of the *Postcommunion,* a venerable companion prayer to

Collect and *Secret.* Like them, it varies in conformity to the particular Mass which is being said. This prayer states in definite terms our wish that the fruits of the Sacrifice may remain in us. Herein lies the conclusion of the act of receiving the Holy Communion.

However, these perspectives are somewhat enlarged by four liturgical acts which now take place. Just as the Mass is drawing to its end, and we are about to take up the work of our daily lives in the midst of cares and danger, the Church reminds us that we must live under the Hand of God, and that as a matter of fact it is under His Hand that we will be guided and protected. In this way the whole essence of the Mass will be, in a sense, incorporated into our being and continued in our daily lives. The *Oratio super populum,* or Prayer said over the people (which is now in use only on week-days from Ash Wednesday until the Wednesday of Holy Week), is of Oriental institution, and it recalls to each one of us, as we listen to its clauses of blessing, that we are all God's children. The *Ite Missa est,* or formulary of dismissal, can be explained as being a solemn announcement of the conclusion of the service, but it also gives notice that our individual service of God is but beginning: the word *missio* can be rendered not only as "dismissal," but also as "mission."[1] By the *Placeat* (which Pius V caused to be inserted in his Missal in the sixteenth century) we are bidden to a realization of the omnipresent Triune God in whose name the final *Blessing* is now invoked upon us. In a beautiful litur-

gical gesture, the celebrant raises his hands on high as though he would draw down from heaven the Grace which now goes forth with us to guard and to guide us. In earlier days this benediction was thought to be so solemn and so important an act that it was only the bishop who could exercise it until as late as the eleventh century.

MY LORD, I beg that You will keep alive in the depths of my heart the thought of this Mass at which I have assisted: grant that I may not look upon it as just another passing hour in a busy life; for it is truly a means by which Your Grace has come to me, and it has given me an opportunity to unite myself more intimately to You.

Do not cast me off, but grant that I may know Your guiding hand to be ever with me: just as in those far-off days You led Your chosen people by the sign of the cloud, so now I beg that you will guide and sustain me by keeping Your presence constantly alive in my thoughts.

And grant that I myself may never turn aside from You: make me always mindful that You are ever present to me as the One reality that no man can overlook. I wish always to seek and to find Your purpose for me in the outward events of my life as well as in those secret encounters whereby I feel my destiny to be shaped.

I beg that my life may be nourished by faith, motivated by love, enlightened by hope, so that I may meet both happiness and trials without losing my sense of reliance upon You; grant that Your Grace may increase within me, and around me, so that all my life may be a prolongation of this Mass and of my union with You.

XXX

In the Glory of the Word

THE LAST GOSPEL

The priest now goes to the left side of the Altar where he reads the Last Gospel after having made the sign of the Cross upon the table and upon himself. This is a late addition to the Mass: the primitive liturgies knew it not, and it is only since the thirteenth century that we find it in the Missals. The custom is an outgrowth of popular piety founded on devotion to Holy Writ. The text which is most frequently used[1] is the Prologue to the Fourth Gospel, that rhythmic hymn with which St. John opens his book as though to give expression to the spiritual life which welled up inexhaustibly within him. The Christians of the Middle Ages held these words in notable veneration; and even in our own time they are said by country people as a sort of exorcism when they wish for fair weather or when they are distressed by a storm. It was an inspired act of Pius V to make this the concluding part of the Mass. How beautifully does the liturgical drama

end by thus opening to us the doors of infinity. Although there is no passage in the Gospel which is more direct, there is none which conveys a sense of greater mystery. The Word which presided at the beginning of all things, the Word in whom lies the origin of creation, that Word by whom all being has life and who is the bright cause of our power to transcend our own limitations, is one with the real Person whose humanity defies our feeble understanding—Christ Our Lord, God who has taken upon Himself our flesh. In the face of such a mystery, man's spirit is dumb and his intellect falls back: it is for his faith to speak. Only because the Word was made flesh and dwelt among us have we been able to know His Glory. As we come to the end of the Mass we are left with the consolation which this truth gives us, in the certainty that it is by the Word—which is Christ—that our own path through life is made known to us.

As NOW, once more, I walk the path of daily life,
Again take up its tasks and duties vexing,
True Light of Light, I call on You for light;
Increate Word; Reason for all being and all becoming:

No more than earthly life can flourish sunless
Could I, lacking You, live without the strength You impart;
As the moon of the sun, I am no more than a feeble reflection
Of Glory's provident care inspiring my least flicker of life.

I call upon You in the Majesty of Your Justice;
In You alone shall I find lasting Truth;
From You do I draw undying draughts of Hope,
Watering me with Grace that woos me to know Your Love.

Grant, Word of God, that my strivings may mirror
That unthought of reflection You will me to be;
Grant, that shown by my acts, fulfilled in my heart,
There may shine forth the pure Light of You I dimly discern in the dark.

It is You alone who can answer my questing,
My wish to know why and how this can be;
Yours alone is true knowledge of life:
Speak to my faith when I languish in doubt.

Grant me, O Word my brother, born of a Virgin Mother,
Sharing with me life's sorrows and anguished end,
Grant me, when trustingly I kneel in Your sight,
Grant me to know that in You rests the answer to all that I seek.

Teach me how Majesty put on Mercy's robe
And bridged by the Cross the great chasm that set us apart:
May Your Blood be not shed in vain; save me, my God;
Let the Word of Your Love resound in my heart.

147

Translator's Annotations

[1] The reference is to the manuscript discovered in 1884 by Gamurrini, the authorship and the provenance of which appear to have been settled by Dom Férotin (cf. *La Révue des Questions Historiques,* October, 1903) and by Dom Fernand Cabrol in his "Études sur la Peregrinatio Silviae" in the great *Dictionnaire d'Archéologie Chrétienne et de Liturgie* (Paris, Letouzey et Ané).

[2] The original text of the *Gloria* is, like that of the *Kyrie,* in Greek. It is extant in two variant forms. One is found in the *Codex Alexandrinus* of the Sacred Scriptures, while the other is part of that curious Syriac document, the so-called *Apostolic Constitutions* (VII, 47). It seems that the Alexandrine Codex has preserved the original, and that the other version is an Arianist (or, at least, an Appolinarist) recension. There are also a number of Latin versions of the *Gloria* which differ slightly from that in our present Missals; see the interesting synoptic table in Dr. F. E. Warren's edition of the old *Bangor Antiphonary,* II; pp. 76–77, (London: Henry Bradshaw Society, 1895; publication no. 10). Cf. also the summation of the history of the use of the *Gloria* in E. G. Cuthbert F. Atchley: *Ordo Romanus Primus* (London: The De La More Press, 1905) pp. 71–72.

CHAPTER VI

[1] The reference is, of course, to the usage at Low Mass; in a chanted Mass, except on days of penitence or when the *Requiem* is celebrated, the congregation observe the primitive attitude of prayer and stand in humble supplication before the Lord.

[2] There has recently appeared, in the series *Études Liturgiques; Collection dirigée par le Centre de Pastorale Liturgique* a most interesting and valuable work which no one who wishes to know the origin, usage, and meaning of these wonderful prayers can afford to neglect. Cf. Dom P. Bruylants, O.S.B.: *Les Oraisons du Missel Romain; Texte et Histoire,* 2 vols. (Louvain: Centre de Documentation et d'Information Liturgiques, Abbaye du Mont-César, 1952).

CHAPTER VII

[1] Dom Botte reminds us that by this term the New Testament writers (as, e.g. Luke 16: 16, 29, 31) intended to signify the whole of the Older Testament. Cf. Bernard Botte & Christine Mohrmann: *L'Ordinaire de la Messe* (Paris: Éditions du Cerf; Louvain: Abbaye du Mont-César, 1953) p. 67, n. 5.

[2] M. Daniel-Rops writes of course with particular reference to the readings preparatory to the old *Missa Praesanctificatorum;* but this feature is preserved in the re-formed service for Good Friday issued according to the Decree of the Sacred Congregation of Rites of November 16, 1955. Here the readings are actually one from *Osee* (6: 1–6), a second from *Exodus* (12: 1–11), and the *Passion* according to St. John (18: 1–40 and 19: 1–42), so that one might say that an even better illustration of the author's description of the more ancient readings is provided by the Mass formulary of the Saturday of the Advent Ember Days where we find a Prophetic reading (sections being provided from Isaias 35: 1–7; 40: 9–11; 45: 1–8; and from Daniel 3: 47–51), a passage from an Apostolic Letter (Paul's second Epistle to the Thessalonians, 2: 1–8), and then the Gospel pericope (Luke 3: 1–6).

CHAPTER X

[1] It is usual to ascribe this adoption to the instance of the Emperor Henry II who came to Rome in the days of Benedict VIII (1012–1024). Berno, abbot of Reichenau, states that when the Emperor asked the Romans why they did not recite the Creed at Mass after the Gospel, he met the reply that inasmuch as the Church of Rome had never been tainted by heresy they had no need to recite the Creed. The Emperor, however, persisted and finally won the consent of the Pope that the Creed be sung at public Masses. Cf. E. G. C. F. Atchley: *Ordo Romanus Primus, with introduction and notes* (London: The De La More Press, 1905) p. 80, citing Berno of Reichenau: *De quibusdam rebus ad missae officium spectantibus libellus,* cap. ii, in J. Cochlaeus: *Speculum Missae* (Venice, 1572) fol. 166. On the rôle of Charlemagne and his great liturgist, Alcuin, in the use of the Creed at Mass, see the recent work of Gerald Ellard, S.J.: *Master Alcuin, Liturgist; a partner of our piety* (Chicago: Loyola University Press, 1956) pp. 184–188.

[2] The old principles governing the use of the Creed at Mass which were in effect when M. Daniel-Rops wrote these words have, as Dr. J. B. O'Connell notes, been *maintained, but somewhat differently applied* by the new rubrics of 1955 (S. R. C. 23 March 1955 in *Acta Apostolicae Sedis,* April 20–22, 1955; pp. 218–224). The Creed is now directed to be said on all fifty-two Sundays, on seventy movable and on nine fixed feasts, on days within the octaves of Christmas, Easter, and Pentecost, and on first class feasts of Patron, Titular, or Founder. The "Messes des vastes assemblées" of the text (here translated as "Masses which particularly concern the whole Christian community") may be taken as identical with the "Missae votivae pro publica causa" of the general rubrics of the Missal (cf. *Missale Romanum:* Rubricae generales, cap. xi & Additiones et variationes in Rubricas, cap. VII, par. 3); and these no longer have the Creed *unless* they are sung Masses. One change made by the new rubrics, which some liturgists may regret, is the deprivation of the feast of St. Mary Magdalene (July 22) of its right to the Creed, formerly enjoyed in virtue of being the day of the *Apostola Apostolorum.* Cf. J. B. O'Connell: *Simplifying the Rubrics of the Roman Breviary and Missal; text of the Decree "Cum nostra," with an English version and a commentary* (London: Burns & Oates, 1955) pp. 67–68.

CHAPTER XIV

[1] Dom Botte points out that in the Sacramentaries of the medieval period are found many prayers beginning *"Suscipe, Sancta Trinitas . . ."* He thinks them to be "of Gallican origin;" for, as he says, "the old Roman liturgy always directed prayer to the Father, not to the Trinity."—D. Bernard Botte, O.S.B. & Christine Mohrmann: *L'Ordinaire de la Messe; texte critique, traduction, et études* (Paris: Les Éditions du Cerf, 1953) p. 73, n. 1. In this connection it is interesting to recall how late Rome was in admitting into her liturgical calendar a special festival in honor of the Trinity.

[2] This interesting feature of the old Lyonnais rite was preserved in the revision that liturgy underwent in the time of Msgr. Antoine de Malvin de Montazet, (archbishop of Lyon 1758–1788). Cf. *Missale sanctae Lugdunensis ecclesiae, primae Galliarum sedis* (Lyon: A. de La Roche, 1771) p. 350. This is a usage also in accord with certain old manuscripts, e.g. the ninth-century Sacramentary of Saint-Thierry, *Reims* 213 (E. 320) [Martène: *De antiquis Ecclesiae ritibus,* I, c.4, art. 12 Ordo IX], and the eleventh-century Sacramentary of Saint-Denis, *Paris, Bibl. Nat. lat.* 9436 [Martène: *loc.*

cit., Ordo V]; cf. B. Botte & C. Mohrmann: *L'Ordinaire de la Messe* (Paris: Les Éditions du Cerf, 1953) p. 72, n. c.

CHAPTER XV

[1] Cf. VI, *supra.*

[2] The Latin word *secernere*, of which *secreta* is the past participle, means *to separate, to set apart from.*

CHAPTER XVI

[1] There has been much discussion among scholars concerning the most just translation and the exact significance of the word *Praefatio.* Cf. the interesting and suggestive summary of opposed (and, at time, complementary) views of the matter which is given by Dom Benedict Steuart in his recent book, *The Development of Christian Worship: an outline of liturgical history* (London: Longmans, Green and Co., 1953) esp. pp. 92–96.

[2] That these improvisations were at times more spontaneous than judicious is sufficiently indicated by Msgr. Duchesne (cf. his *Christian Worship;* tr. by M. L. McClure; fifth edition [London: Society for Promoting Christian Knowledge, 1949] pp. 141–143); and we may well be thankful, for the decorum of our worship, that we nowadays have a book in which what is to be declaimed is set down beforehand.

[3] When, in 1738, the archbishop of Paris, Msgr. de Vintimille du Luc, issued his magnificent revision of the Missal, he wisely justified the increased number of Prefaces which marked it by the observation that he thus recalled an earlier day in the Roman liturgy when "almost every Mass had its own proper Preface." Cf. *Missale Parisiense . . . D. Caroli-Gaspar-Guillelmi de Vintimille Parisiensis Archiepiscopi auctoritate . . . editum . . .* (Paris: A. Le Clere et Cie., 1830) mandatum, p. vi.

CHAPTER XVII

[1] This word has a long history in the Old Testament. Very many translations of the Missal render the expression *Deus Sabaoth* (which is the Hebrew *Jahvé Saba'ot*) as "God of hosts." The general French usage has been "Dieu des armées" (cf. *Livre d'Église Latin-François . . . Imprimé par ordre de Monseigneur l'Arche-*

vêque [Paris: P. G. Le Mercier, 1744] p. lxxv; and *Petit Paroissien . . . de Poitiers* [Poitiers: F.-A. Barbier, 1843] p. 187); but in the new translation of the Mass Ordinary prepared at the instance of the *Centre du Pastorale liturgique* at Paris, the rendering is "Dieu des Forces célestes." D. Botte remarks that although it would seem that in the liturgy of the Mass the "hosts" are chiefly those of angels, the word nevertheless does retain a cosmic significance. Cf. Bernard Botte & Christine Mohrmann: *L'Ordinaire de la Messe* (Paris: Les Éditions du Cerf, 1953) p. 75, n. 8.

CHAPTER XVIII

[1] The exact force of this word in this place is much debated among latter-day liturgiologists (see the summary of opinions advanced in Dom Benedict Steuart's study, *The Development of Christian Worship* [London: Longmans, Green, and Co., 1953] esp. pp. 101–105); and D. Botte goes so far as to declare forthrightly that in fourth-century Latin, *igitur* is no stronger than the Greek post-positive conjunction δε (cf. Botte: op. cit.; p. 75, n. 9), which, as the grammarians commonly tell us, is very often to be entirely omitted in translation; and this is the course which D. Botte has followed in his new French version of the Ordinary of the Mass.

CHAPTER XIX

[1] See, however, note 1, Chapter xxviii (p. 154), where this point is more fully discussed.

[2] Moreover, as D. Botte justly says, "in all liturgies, the recitation of the institution of the Eucharist rests upon a tradition which is independent of the evangelical accounts . . . [but] an effort has been made to blend the two factors into a symmetrical unit, and to find an expression of them which is close to the Gospel text." Cf. Botte: *op. cit.;* p. 81, n. 1.

[3] Cf. "This expression is borrowed from St. Paul and it is to be taken in the Pauline sense: the Eucharist is *the* mystery of the faith, that is to say, it contains and reveals the whole economy of redemption." B. Botte: *op cit.;* p. 81, n. 3.

[4] Perhaps attention may usefully be called here to the very illuminating paper by Professor

Arthur Darby Nock of Harvard in *Mnemosyne,* 1952, on the very wide sense in which the term *sacramentum* (which is the Latin equivalent of the Greek *mysterion*) was used in the fourth century, and to a recent work by H. Rondet, M. Le Landais, A. Lauras, and Ch. Couturier—I refer to their *Études Augustiniennes* (Paris: Aubier, 1953)—wherein is attempted a detailed examination of the meaning of the words *sacramentum* and *mysterium* in the writings of St. Augustine. These terms are found used in that holy Doctor's writings no less than 2279 times, and M. Couturier has classified them according to rite, symbol, or mystery, and has tried to point out their underlying conformity.

⁵ The allusion M. Daniel-Rops makes here is to the candle which, according to the rubrics of the Missal, is to be lit on the Epistle side of the altar by the server at this point in the Mass and not extinguished until after the Communion. Cf. *Missale Romanum; Ritus servandus in celebratione Missae,* viii, 5. Not of universal observance, this rite is generally seen in churches served by the Dominicans and by the Fathers of the Blessed Sacrament, and in some others.

CHAPTER XX

¹ We here touch upon the fascinating question of the *essential nature* of sacrifice and how it is effected, a point which has exercised the attention of theological writers for centuries; cf. the remarks made by D. Benedict Steuart in the introduction to his book already cited; pp. xx-xxiii. The whole question has been suggestively treated in our own day by Père M. de la Taille in his *Mysterium Fidei* (Paris: Beauchesne, 1921; English tr. [by Carroll and Dalton] *The Mystery of Faith* 2 vols., New York: Sheed & Ward, 1940–50), and by M. l'Abbé Lepin in his *L'idée du sacrifice de la messe d'après les théologiens* (Paris, 1926). Cf. also the article, of A. Michel "La Messe chez les théologiens postérieurs au Concile de Trente" in Vacant-Mangenot: *Dictionnaire de Théologic Catholique* (Paris, 1928) X (1); cc. 1143–1316.

CHAPTER XXI

¹ In some manuscript Sacramentaries (as, for example, in that known as the Sacramentary of Saint-Thierry, in the Library at Reims, 213

[E. 320] [cf. Martène: *De antiquis Ecclesiae ritibus,* I, c.4, art. 12, Ordo IX], and in that which is in the Bibliothèque Nationale at Paris under the classification Ms. lat. 9428, both of which date from the ninth century), mention is here made of the Nativity as well. Cf. Botte: *op. cit.,* p. 80, n. 1.

² As, for example, at Lyon, and among the Dominicans, the Carthusians, and the Carmelites. Cf. W. R. Bonniwell: *A History of the Dominican Liturgy* (New York: J. F. Wagner, 1944) pp. 127, 186; Archdale A. King: *Liturgies of the Religious Orders* (Milwaukee, Wisconsin: The Bruce Publishing Co., 1955) pp. 51, 311, 386.

CHAPTER XXII

¹ On both these commemorations consult the fine study of V. L. Kennedy, C.S.B.: *The Saints of the Canon of the Mass* (Rome: Pontificio Istituto di Archaeologia Cristiana, 1938).

CHAPTER XXIII

¹ The reference, in respect to the liturgy as at present constituted (according to the Decree of the S. C. R. of November 16, 1955) is to the *Missa Chrismalis* now directed to be celebrated in Cathedral Churches early on the morning of Maundy Thursday. As far as the "good things" referred to in this great Doxology in the Mass are concerned, cf. *Genesis* I. The question of the precise significance of the terms of this prayer is one which has long agitated liturgiologists, and Msgr. Duchesne has, in his usual masterly fashion, summed up the reasons for believing that these words, *Per quem haec omnia . . . bona, etc.,* indicate the presence here, at one time, of a formulary of benediction of first fruits, (see L. M. O. Duchesne: *Christian Worship;* tr. by M. L. McClure; 5th edition [London: S. P. C. K., 1949] pp. 182–183); but not everyone has been satisfied with this explanation, and some recent writers have even attempted to justify the employment of this strange terminology as *originally* having pertained to the Sacred Elements themselves, (cf. the discussion of late theorizing on this head which is summed up by D. Benedict Steuart in his *The Development of Christian Worship* [London: Longmans, Green & Co., 1953] esp. pp. 159–162 and 185). D. Botte evidently thinks the question insoluble at present, for he

remarks that it is not easy to see whether the words *haec omnia* apply to the objects sometimes blessed at this point in the service or only to the consecrated species. Cf. B. Botte: *op. cit.;* p. 85, n.7.

2 The French custom of ringing a bell at this point in the Mass is not everywhere observed. Where the Roman rubrics are rigidly adhered to and where there flourishes that school of liturgists who are wont to reproach the French Church for "a fondness for overmuch bell-ringing," the Little Elevation passes in silence. The Roman Missal (cf. *Ritus servandus,* IX, 3) says nothing of a bell here; but in the Paris Missal of 1738 we find it expressly stated in words of which those written by M. Daniel-Rops might almost be an echoing translation, *cujus elevationis signum datur pulsatione campanulae.* Cf. *Missale Parisiense . . . D. Caroli-Gaspar-Guillelmi de Vintimille Par. Arch. auctoritate . . . editum* [1738] *necnon . . . D. Hyacinthi-Ludovici de Quélen, Par. Arch. jussu recognitum ac typis denuo mandatum* (Paris: Ad. Le Clere & Cie., 1830) p. 49: *de ritibus in Missa servandis;* cap. II, 67.

CHAPTER XXV

1 It is noteworthy that the prayers at meal times which are said according to monastic custom all have a pronouncedly Eucharistic flavor about them.

2 The reference here is to the rite of the *Sancta* which must not be confused with the rite of the *Fermentum,* although there are interesting analogies between the two. Both were designed to show the unity which underlies the Eucharistic celebration; but while the *fermentum* emphasized this in respect to place, the *Sancta* did so insofar as concerns time. It was anciently customary at Rome that when the priests in charge of the various urban churches were unable to join with the Sovereign Pontiff in the celebration of Mass at the stational church of the day, he would send to them portions of one of the loaves consecrated by him. This, the *fermentum,* exemplified their *unity* with their bishop, a unity which was so stressed by St. Ignatius the Martyr when he wrote to the Church of Smyrna: "Let that Eucharist be esteemed valid which is either offered by the bishop or by him to whom he has given permission." (Cf. W. Jacobson, ed.: *Patrum Apostolicorum quae supersunt* [Oxford, 1863] II, p. 320, cap. xx.) According to the rite of the *Sancta,* a fragment consecrated at a previous Mass was put into the chalice at *Pax Domini* to indicate that there was always the same Sacrifice, the same Eucharist, the same Communion; that the communicants at the Mass being said or sung were united with those at the previous celebration, and so on back through the ages. (Cf. Duchesne: *op. cit.;* Eng. tr.; 5th ed. [1949]; pp. 184–185; also E. G. C. F. Atchley, ed.: *Ordo Romanus Primus* [London: The De La More Press, 1905] pp. 106–109.) It is only in connection with the rite of the *Sancta* that there can be explained the custom (still required by the rubrics governing the celebration of the Solemn Mass) of the subdeacon holding the empty paten wrapped in the humeral veil and raised aloft in reverence, from the time of the offertory until the Pater has been sung; for it appears that anciently the paten held the fragment of the Holy Sacrament destined to serve in the rite of the *Sancta.* It was D. Jean Mabillon, the great seventeenth-century liturgiologist, who elaborated this explanation in his own commentary on *Ordo Romanus primus* (cf. Migne: *Patrologia Latina,* LXXVII, 869–870), and in our own memory it has been sanctioned by the high authority of Msgr. Duchesne (cf. *op. cit.,* supra). Nevertheless, some modern liturgists have expressed considerable reservation in this matter. The Anglican Benedictine, D. Gregory Dix, is content with the consideration that the *provenance* of this rite is Gaul, and that it was introduced into the Roman rite only during the sixth century. (cf. Dix: *The Shape of the Liturgy* [London: Dacre Press, 1945] p. 134); but the Abbot of Mont-César at Louvain, D. Bernard Capelle, is more strongly opposed to the bare notion of such a rite, and he seems to be of the opinion that it had no existence save *in the brain of D. Mabillon.* (cf. B. Capelle in *La Révue Bénédictine,* LIII; pp. 17–22.) A great disadvantage of this new theorizing is that its acceptance would deprive us of any rational explanation for the seemingly excessive reverence with which the subdeacon is still made to treat what is now an empty paten. Cf. the summary of this whole question by D. Benedict Steuart in his *The Development of Christian Worship* (1953); pp. 168–179.

CHAPTER XXVII

[1] D. Botte tells us that the word *judicium* used here often has in liturgical contexts a pejorative sense signifying a condemnatory sentence. It would thus seem to serve as an intensification of the word *condemnationem* which follows it. Cf. Botte & Mohrmann: *op. cit.;* p. 89, n. 1, where a reference is given to John 5: 24; and *ibid.;* p. 90, n.b., where we are bidden to take into account I Cor. 11: 29.

[2] The Dominicans, even today, employ but one of these prayers. Cf. A. A. King: *op. cit.;* p. 388. Fr. Ellard, S.J., has recently summed up the evidence, set forth by D. André Wilmart, which justifies the ascription of these two beautiful prayers to Alcuin. Cf. Gerald Ellard, S.J.: *Master Alcuin, Liturgist; a partner of our piety* (Chicago: Loyola University Press, 1956) pp. 171–173.

CHAPTER XXVIII

[1] D. Benedict Steuart notes that "the whole question of the agape is still very much disputed and liturgical authorities do not agree about its true character nor the method of usage." (Cf. Steuart: *op. cit.;* p. 6). Msgr. Duchesne tells us that the Eucharistic celebration at first followed an ordinary repast partaken of in common, as may be seen from St. Paul's first Epistle to the Corinthians; "but," as Duchesne remarks, "the custom allowed of the introduction of too many inconveniences to be lasting," and "the liturgical Agape disappeared, or nearly so, within less than a hundred years after the first preaching of the Gospel." (Cf. Duchesne: *op. cit.;* p. 49, n. 1.) Of Eastern institution and observance, the *Agapé* seems never to have flourished at Rome.

CHAPTER XXIX

[1] Attractive as this idea certainly is, and spiritually suggestive as many might find it, it must be admitted that it fails to satisfy the requirements of scientific philology. Apparently, it was first proposed by Herr Dr. Kristensen in his study of *the sacrament of mission* ("Het sacrament van de uitzending, missa," in *Mededelingen der Koninkl. Nederl. Academie van Wetenschappen, afd. Letterkunde,* 1949; pp. 3–15) but was shown to be based on insufficient evidence by M. l'Abbé J. Mogenet in his article "Ite missa est," in *La Révue diocésaine de Tournai,* 6 (1951); pp. 297–303. D. Botte sums up the history of attempts to explain this formulary in the excursus upon it with which he closes his fine work on the Ordinary of the Mass. (Cf. Botte: *L'Ordinaire de la Messe* [Paris, 1953] pp. 145–149.) And more recently M. l'Abbé Amiot acidly points out that "those modern commentators who with the best of intentions suggest that *Ite missa est* means: 'Go; it is now that your own mission is beginning' are expressing an idea which is sound enough in itself but are doing so in a way calculated to cast suspicion upon their knowledge of liturgical Latin." (Cf. François Amiot: *Histoire de la Messe* [Paris: Arthème Fayard, 1956] p. 120.)

CHAPTER XXX

[1] Formerly a somewhat complicated set of rubrics regulated the variations which could take place in this part of the Mass, for since the first codification of those rules under Pius V a definite procedure has had to be followed in choosing a particular pericope to be read as part of the commemoration made of a feast or of a special feria. These rules were clarified under Pius X, and again in 1922 by a special decree (N. 4369) of the Sacred Congregation of Rites. However, the complications were drastically reduced by the decree "Cum nostra" of March 23, 1955 (published in *Acta Apostolicae Sedis* 47 [20–22 Apr. 1955] pp. 218–224) simplifying the rubrics of the Roman Breviary and Missal, and now the Prologue to St. John's Gospel is used as a last Gospel for every Mass except the third Mass of Christmas Day and Masses said privately on Palm Sunday, i.e., at all Masses on that day except the one attached to the blessing of palms and the procession.

ALASTAIR GUINAN

ABOUT THIS BOOK

AND THE MEN WHO MADE IT

HENRI DANIEL-ROPS was born Henri Jules Charles Petiot, January 19, 1901, at Épinal (Vosges), France, the grandson of peasants and the son of Colonel Charles Petiot, an artillery officer, and Odile Grosperrin. A dark-haired, slender, serious student, he majored simultaneously in law, geography and history at the University of Grenoble, winning the equivalent of a Master's degree in each subject and gaining his "agrégation" (slightly higher than a Ph.D.) from the University of Lyons before he was twenty-one. A year later he received his "habilitation," teaching as a "professeur agrégé" at the University. He subsequently taught history at the lycée at Charbéry, then taught at Amiens, and from 1930 until he retired from teaching in 1945, he was a professor at Neuilly. He adopted the nom de plume of Daniel-Rops for his first book—a volume of essays published in 1926—and has used it for all of his prolific writings. His more than seventy books include twenty novels, and the other writings are historical studies,

works in the arts and sciences, poetry, and children's books. His writings have brought him many honors, including election to the Académie Française in 1955, the youngest member at the time. Other honors include Commander of the Order of Saint Gregory the Great in 1949 (conferred by Pope Pius XII, who is an ardent reader of his works) and the Grand Cross of that order in 1956; Commander of the Order of Christ (Portugal); Knight of the Legion of Honor; winner of the Académie Française Grand Prix de la Littérature as well as its Prix Paul Flat and Prix Alfred Née. He holds honorary degrees from many institutions of higher learning including the Université de Montréal, Montreal, Canada. In addition to his writing, he lectures weekly and answers up to twenty letters daily from people who write with problems. A painstaking workman in his writing, he researches with fine-tooth-comb care and has a library at his home, Eau Vive, at Tresserve (Savoy) of more than 10,000 volumes. His greatest success was *Jesus* and His Times (Dutton, 1954) which took him three years to write, working daily from 7 a.m. to 1 p.m., his door shut and telephone disconnected. The work was translated into fourteen languages and has sold more than a half-million copies. He is a regular contributor to Revue des Deux Mondes, Nouvelle Revue Française, La France Catholique, Témoignage Chrétien, and La Bataille, as well as the editor of four series of books, including the *Twentieth Century Encyclopedia of Catholicism*. He contributes to various newspapers, edits a popular monthly, Ecclesia, and publishes an intellectual quarterly. His intensity of feeling for humanity was mirrored in the three years of research alone he spent preparing to write *Histoire Sainte* published in English both as *Sacred History* and *Israel and the Ancient World* (Longmans, Green, 1949). It was a work inspired by the Nazi libels against the Jews, and he felt he was "working against time to disabuse the world of these calumnies." Hardly had the work been set in type and 14,000 copies printed when the Gestapo raided the publisher's plant and destroyed the book plates. They failed to find the finished books, however, and the work was reset and reprinted after the war. Other of his books published in English are: *Misted Mirror* (Knopf, New York, 1931), *Two Men in Me* (Rockwell, Chicago, 1931), *The Poor and Ourselves* (Burns, Oates, London, 1938), *Flaming Sword* (Cassell, London, 1941), *Death, Where Is Thy Victory?* (Cassell, London, 1946), *Where Angels Pass* (Cassell, London, 1950), *Saint Paul: Apostle of Nations* (Fides, Chicago, 1953), *Book of Books* (Kenedy, New York, 1956), *Book of Life* (Kenedy, New York, 1956), and *Cathedral and Crusade* (Dutton, New York, 1957). In 1923 he was married to Madelaine Bouvier and they have an adopted son, Francis. When not occupied with his writing, he works around his garden and makes up stories to tell to his god-daughter, but, he says: "I believe I would die if I could no longer write."

FULTON JOHN SHEEN was born May 8, 1895, at El Paso, Illinois, one of four sons of Newton Morris and Delia (Fulton) Sheen. He was baptized Peter and took the name of John at confirmation, later adopting his mother's maiden name. His father was a farmer, but the family later moved to Peoria, Ill., where he attended St. Mary's School and Spalding Institute from which he was graduated in 1913. He received his A.B. and M.A. degrees from St. Viator College, Bourbonnais, Ill., where he first tasted the pleasures of speaking and writing as a member of the college debating team and newspaper staff. He completed his theological studies at St. Paul's Seminary, St. Paul, Minn., and was ordained to the priesthood for the Diocese of Peoria, September 20, 1919. A year later he obtained his degrees of Bachelor of Sacred Theology and Bachelor of Canon Law from the Catholic University of America, and went to the University of Louvain, Belgium, where he was awarded a Ph.D. in 1923. He also attended the Sorbonne in Paris and the Collegio Angelico in Rome. In 1924 he received his Doctorate of Sacred Theology in Rome, and a year later while teaching dogmatic theology at St. Edmund's College, Ware, England, he was made an Agrégé en Philosophie by Louvain and awarded that university's Cardinal Mercier International Philosophy Award. His honorary degrees include LL.D., Litt.D. and L.H.D. On his return to the United States, he served as a curate of St. Patrick's Church in Peoria and joined the faculty of the Catholic University of America, Washington, D. C., in 1926 as a philosophy of religion instructor, later being promoted to a full professorship. In June, 1934, he was appointed Papal Chamberlain and was elevated the following year to Domestic Prelate. He was consecrated Bishop on June 11, 1951, a year after he became National Director of the Society for the Propagation of the Faith. As a preacher he has been heard by millions in the United States, Canada and England, through the media of radio and television. A prolific writer, he is author of two syndicated columns: "God Love You" for the Catholic press, and "Bishop Sheen Speaks," for the secular press; and is editor of two magazines: Worldmission, a quarterly review, and Mission, a bi-monthly. The popularity of his radio and television programs can be judged from the fact that his daily mail as a result of these programs has reached as much as ten thousand letters in a single day—about one-third of them from non-Catholics. The largest single delivery of mail after a program was thirty thousand letters. He conducted the first religious service ever telecast, served as narrator for a March of Time film, and has had his sermons issued in record album form. His interests are wide and as well as serving on such organizations as the Catholic Literary Guild and the American Catholic Philosophical Society, he is an active member of the Mediaeval Academy and the American Geographical Association. The long list of his books started with publication of *God and Intelligence in Modern Philosophy* (Longmans, Green, 1925). This was followed by *Religion Without God* (Longmans, Green, 1928), *The Life of All Living* (Century, 1929), *The Divine Romance* (Century, 1930), *Old Errors and New Labels* (Century, 1931), *Moods and Truths* (Century, 1932), *The Way of the Cross* (Appleton-Century, 1933), *Seven Last Words* (Appleton-Century, 1933), *The Eternal Galilean* (Appleton-Century, 1934), *The Philosophy of Science* (Bruce, 1934), *The Mystical Body of Christ* (Sheed and Ward, 1935), *Calvary and the Mass* (Kenedy, 1936), *The Moral Universe* (Bruce, 1936), *The Cross and the Beatitudes* (Kenedy, 1937), *The Cross and the Crisis* (Bruce, 1938), *Liberty, Equality and Fraternity* (Macmillan, 1938), *The Rainbow of Sorrow* (Kenedy, 1938), *Victory Over Vice* (Kenedy, 1939), *Freedom Under God* (Bruce, 1940), *Whence Come Wars* (Sheed and Ward, 1940), *The Seven Virtues* (Kenedy, 1940), *For God and Country* (Kenedy, 1941), *A Declaration of Dependence* (Bruce, 1941), *God and War* (Kenedy, 1942), *The Divine Verdict* (Kenedy, 1943), *The Armor of God* (Kenedy, 1943), *Philosophies at War* (Scribner's, 1943), *Seven Words to the Cross* (Kenedy, 1944), *Seven Pillars of Peace* (Scribner's, 1944), *Love One Another* (Kenedy, 1944), *Seven Words of Jesus and Mary* (Kenedy, 1945), *Preface to Religion* (Kenedy, 1946), *Characters of the Passion* (Kenedy, 1946), *Jesus, Son of Mary* (McMullen, 1947), *Communism and the Conscience of the West* (Bobbs, Merrill, 1948), *Philosophy of Religion* (Appleton-Century-Crofts, 1948), *Peace of Soul* (McGraw-Hill, 1949), *Lift Up Your Heart* (McGraw-Hill, 1950), *Three to Get Married* (Appleton-Century-Crofts, 1951), *The World's First Love* (McGraw-Hill, 1952), *Life Is Worth Living, First Series* (McGraw-Hill, 1953), *Life Is Worth Living, Second Series* (McGraw-Hill, 1954), *The Life of Christ* (McGraw-Hill, 1954), *The Way to Happiness* (Garden City, 1954), *Life Is Worth Living, Third Series* (McGraw-Hill, 1955), *The Way to Inner Peace* (Garden City, 1955),

Yousuf Karsh and Bishop Sheen

God Love You (Garden City, 1955), *Thinking Life Through* (Garden City, 1955), *The True Meaning of Christmas* (McGraw-Hill, 1955), *Life Is Worth Living, Fourth Series* (McGraw-Hill, 1956), *Thoughts for Daily Living* (Garden City, 1956), *Life Is Worth Living, Fifth Series* (McGraw-Hill, 1957). He is Auxiliary Bishop of New York.

Yousuf Karsh was born December 23, 1908, at Mardin, Armenia, and left for Canada at the age of fifteen during the Turkish massacres. Son of an import-export entrepreneur and grandson of an engraver, he went to stay with an uncle, A. G. Nakash, who owned a photography studio in Sherbrooke, Quebec. He took an interest in the art of the camera and was sent by his uncle to Boston to study. After several years in the United States he went to open his own studio in Canada's capital, where within a few years he was photographing the cream of society and leaders of government. When war broke out in 1939, Ottawa became a center of Allied war activity and "Karsh of Ottawa" became a familiar signature on the portraits of some of the world's greatest leaders. His famous portrait of Winston Churchill in 1941 rocketed him to fame as the world's greatest portrait photographer, and that photograph along with seventy-four others, taken in all parts of the world in the four years that followed, went into making his only book, *Faces of Destiny* (Ziff-Davis, 1946). Still a world traveler, he keeps cameras and equipment at studios in London, Paris and New York, as well as in Ottawa, and usually carries a set of traveling equipment that weighs a minimum of 250 pounds. He always uses a white camera, finding that the traditional black is too depressing, and his focusing cloth varies in color with his own mood—though it is most often of red velvet with a gold satin lining. Groups of his portraits form part of the permanent collections of such museums as the Brooklyn Museum Department of Photography and the Museum of Modern Art in New York, Eastman House, Rochester, N. Y., The Art Institute of Chicago, and the Huntington Library, San Marino, Cal. In acknowledgment of his contribution to Canadian art and culture he received one of the first Canadian Citizenship Certificates in January, 1947, when Parliament passed a law creating Canadian citizenship. He is actively interested in Canadian theatre and met Solange Gauthier, whom he married in 1939, when she was acting with the Ottawa Drama League. She serves frequently as model for his work and shares his love for gardening and tennis.